A BEGINNER'S GUIDE TO WINNING BIG BUCKS AT LITTLE GAMES!

How to Beat Low-Limit Poker

D1009883

ABOUT THE AUTHORS

Shane Smith is widely regarded as one of the greatest poker writers and one of the top low-limit players. In addition to being the author of the best-selling classics, *Omaha High-Low: How to Win at the Lower Limits* and *Poker Tournament Tips from the Pros*, as well as several other titles, Shane has collaborated with world champions and some of the greatest players including Tom McEvoy, T.J. Cloutier, Roy West, Brad Daugherty, Linda Johnson and the late Byron "Cowboy" Wolford. She has also acted as the editor for two gaming magazines, and placed in the money or won countless poker tournaments.

Tom McEvoy, the 1983 World Champion of Poker, has won four gold bracelets at the World Series of Poker and is the best-selling author of a dozen poker books.

Dedicated to the memory of three generous poker players and authors whose enduring friendship and support inspired and helped me immensely:

Bill "Bulldog" Sykes, low-limit Omaha player and humorous raconteur, who was one of the original *Card Player* columnists and the author of *Poker: Las Vegas Style*.

Tex Sheahan, low-limit hold'em tournament player and loving family man who, with only a high school education, became "The Dean" of vintage *Card Player* columnists, and the author of *Wins, Places and Pros*, and *Secrets of Winning Poker*.

Byron "Cowboy" Wolford, champion rodeo calf roper in the 1950s, who won a WSOP gold bracelet in 1991 in limit hold'em, and wrote *Cowboys, Gamblers & Hustlers*, his memoir of the early days of both rodeo and poker.

How to Beat Low-Limit Poker

Shane Smith
& Tom McEvoy

CARDOZA PUBLISHING

Cardoza Publishing is the foremost gaming and gambling publisher in the world with a library of more than 200 up-to-date and easy-to-read books and strategies. These authoritative works are written by the top experts in their fields and with more than 10,000,000 books in print, represent the best-selling and most popular gaming books anywhere.

Visit our web site (www.cardozapub.com) or write us
for a full list of books, advanced and computer strategies.

CARDOZA PUBLISHING

PO Box 1500 Cooper Station, New York, NY 10276
Phone (800)577-WINS
email: cardozapub@aol.com
www.cardozapub.com

Table of Contents

FOREWORD

by **T.J. Cloutier**
Poker Champion, Author, Member of the Poker Hall of Fame

Shane Smith's books have been helping players beat low-limit poker games for the past decade or so, starting with *Omaha High-Low Poker* in 1991 and followed by *Poker Tournament Tips from the Pros* the next year. Now Smith has updated, expanded and improved *How to Beat Low-Limit Poker* with proven strategies and insider information on how to beat today's most popular poker games at the limits that most people play.

Believe me, all of us—including McEvoy and Brunson and Negreanu—started playing poker at the lower limits until we got good enough to move up the money ladder. Sure, I've won some $10,000 tournaments, but I certainly didn't start out at those stakes. The first tournament I ever played cost $300 to enter and I didn't come close to winning it. The first time I played Texas hold'em, the blinds were $5/$10.

After some hard lessons that I learned by the seat of my pants, I started making more money at poker than I was making as a roughneck in the oil fields around Dallas. It wouldn't have taken me so long to learn how to win if I'd had even one poker book to help me understand the most important aspects of the game. But there were no books, no software programs, no Internet free-money practice rooms, nothing except sitting down at a poker table with your case money in front of you gambling against guys with more money and more experience than you.

Sometimes I look back at those days and wonder how I made it through. And how I ever became the author of five poker books and the winner of six World Series of Poker gold bracelets. Then I remember all the good advice I've gotten along the way, advice that helped me leave those dusty back-room games in Texas and move up the ladder in the major-league tournament world.

I heartily recommend that if you want to learn how to play better poker and win some money while you're enjoying the game, read Shane Smith's advice in this book. You won't find a better low-limit poker teacher anywhere.

1. INTRODUCTION

"You can't make money at low-limit poker," I frequently hear people say, but they're wrong. I make money, several of my friends make money, and so can you if you are a skilled low-limit player. How much money you win depends on several things: how good a player you are; how good (or hopefully, bad) your opponents are; the betting limits of the game; the house rake; and that other dimension of poker that theorists sometimes downplay—luck.

Winning at low-limit casino poker requires a distinctive set of skills, not the least of which is (ugh!) discipline. Because I have a built-in aversion to that word, I prefer to use the term "self-control." Somehow, it feels better and I don't hear my mother's voice in it. Actually there are several other important concepts to keep in mind if you are an aspiring low-limit poker player. Let's take a look at how playing low-limit poker differs from playing at the higher limits.

First, low-limit poker is "showdown" poker. Most hands are going to be played all the way through to the final card. This is why starting out with really good cards is so important. Secondly, most pots are played multiway. More players enter the pot in low-limit games than they do in higher-limit games. For this reason, the drawing hands in low-limit poker go up in value. With more people in each pot, players are getting better odds to draw to straights and flushes than they would in higher-limit poker where fewer people come into pots. Drawing hands contribute to the greater number of players that stay in to the showdown.

Also, most people begin their poker adventures by playing low-limit poker. Therefore the skill level in low-limit games is not as high as it is in higher-limit games. Most beginners play straight-forward poker, so there is far less deceptive play in the low-limit games.

Actually, when I think it through, if you're into action poker, if you like to play a lot of hands, and if you prefer a more relaxed play-ing environment, low-limit poker is a great place to be! Especially if you enjoy earning while you're learning—and I firmly believe you'll be able to do exactly that after reading this book.

2. ARE YOU DIVING, SURVIVING, STRIVING OR THRIVING?

Now let's move right along to exploring the phases you may experience while learning how to earn both pleasure and profit at low-limit poker. To paraphrase Robert Schuller's catchy alliteration in *Possibility Thinking,* poker players progress through four stages in the lose-win cycle: diving, surviving, striving, and thriving.

DIVING

Low-limit kitchen table players accustomed to a loose, friendly game of down-home poker often begin playing poker by taking a bath at $2/$4 stud, or drowning on the river in $4/$8 Omaha high-low, or getting eaten by the sharks in $2/$4/$8 Texas hold'em. Casino poker is not always casual, friendly or loose, but it can be fun if you know how to win at it. It's just that so few casual players have learned the tricks of the trade—so they take a dive into its muddy waters and their bankrolls take a bath.

Conversations I have had with many Las Vegas poker players verify this fact: It takes a while to adjust to low-limit poker in public cardrooms. Most players tell me it requires from about six months to a year to begin to get the hang of it—translated, that means start making money at it. Basic Truth: Low-limit players in the casinos of Las Vegas are the toughest you will find anywhere. My earnings took an initial dive of around 70 percent when I first moved to Vegas from Los Angeles. It took me about six months to rescue my money and bring it back to the winning level to which I had become accustomed in the cardrooms of Southern California (where they play loose, folks, very loose).

The bottom line is my bankroll took a hit when I first began playing in the "big leagues" of low-limit casino poker. But I've learned a few things since dragging my bankroll through the monetary mud. In this book, you'll get a chance to find out what I've learned, and it won't cost you a single farthing (a far sight less than it cost me!).

And it will cost you a whole lot less than John Bonetti invested in his "lessons." The winner of numerous *World Series of Poker* and other major tournament events, Bonetti admits to once having been a *diver*: "For three or four years, I supported most of the hold'em players in Houston. They used to wait for me to show up. I *made* the games."

Don Gay

"Here's a bull that can make you well."

World Champion Bull Rider

Divers play too many hands, take too many draws, call too many raises—and lose more money than they have to. Novices are often shy, hesitant to ask questions of the dealer, meek in placing their bets. You sometimes hear them say, "I'm just here for some fun. I don't expect to win any money." And sure enough, they don't!

SURVIVING

As rookies at the low-limit casino games, many poker players hide out in their survival cocoons, playing very careful poker. They may be former divers who have decided to get with it and quit losing money. Or maybe they are so afraid of losing or perhaps of looking stupid, they play tentative poker. Some authors refer to that style of play as tight-timid.

"The first goal of a low-limit player is to play *not to lose*, in contrast to the higher limit player who is playing to win," said Tex Sheahan, author of *Secrets of Winning Poker*. Tex's opinion is contrary to what poker is all about in some people's minds—winning. But survivors at low-limit poker must learn to not lose before they can learn how to win.

To survive at low-limit poker, you must do at least three things:

1. Play tighter than your opponents;
2. Determine how good your hand is compared to your opponents' hands;
3. Know when to fold.

Is it possible for a novice to win a reasonable amount of money playing low-limit poker? Bill "Bulldog" Sykes said, "This may surprise many of you, but the answer is a qualified yes. You don't have to be an expert or a world-class player to win in a poker game. You only have to be a shade better than the people you are playing against."

SURVIVAL SKILL #1
Play fewer hands than you want to play
Don't succumb to your natural instinct for action.

SURVIVAL SKILL #2
Continually ask yourself, "What is the best possible hand at this moment?

Given the flop (in hold'em and Omaha) or the board (in seven-card stud), ask yourself what's the best hand out there?" Then ask, "Do I hold the best hand or have a draw to it?" The answers to these questions are what help you find out the relative strength of your hand.

SURVIVAL SKILL #3
Fold your hand when you believe you are beaten

It makes no difference whether you're on the flop, turn or river in hold'em, or on third through seventh streets in seven-card stud. Many low-limit players stay in a hand too long—they chase in hold'em or draw dead in stud. In *High-Low Split Poker*, Ray Zee states that low-limit and high-limit poker are often two different games. "Play somewhat tighter and more conservatively if you choose to play in the bigger games," he recommends.

If tight, conservative, yet aggressive play with a good hand is such a winning combination at the higher limits, why not give yourself an edge by practicing those strategies in the low limit games?

You can be sure that some of your casino poker opponents are playing that way because not all low-limit players are beginners—in fact, very few casino poker players are new to poker. Some are advanced players who sit in low-limit games because they don't have sufficient bankrolls for the higher limits, or because they don't feel comfortable playing higher than $5/$10 limit poker. Some are retirees on fixed incomes, grinding out $40-a-day wins. Others may even be former high-limit players who have gone bust and have stepped down a notch to rebuild their bankrolls. Bill Smith, who won the World Series of Poker championship in 1985, used to play regularly in the $4/$8 hold'em game at the Gold Coast casino in Las Vegas. He had retired from high-limit poker, was getting older, felt less stress at the lower limits and he was a winning player at those limits.

You'll find all types of players in low-limit casino poker games so if you have a choice, try to find a table at which five or more players are in most pots and there isn't much raising going on. These types of games are called "loose passive" and are ideal for beginners (in fact, for any player). Ask the floor person for a table change if your game doesn't match this description, although in most hometown cardrooms that spread only one to three games, that may be impossible. In that case, either get lucky or go home early!

STRIVING

Striving to become a better poker player is always a serious player's first priority, even top-cabin competitors. Bonetti explains how he became a winner: "I picked up some poker books and read them faithfully every day and night, and finally began to see where I was making my mistakes."

It isn't always the things you do right that lead to a win. It is also the things that you *don't do wrong*. Ask yourself, "Where are the leaks in my game? What do I need to do to plug them?" Strivers must learn to recognize their own weaknesses before they can improve their play, increase their wins and move up to *thrive* status.

Here are some techniques that strivers can benefit from:

1. Since low-limit games are usually looser than high-limit games, if they're playing loose, you play a shade tighter.
2. During the hands you aren't playing, observe the playing habits of your opponents: How many pots do they enter? What seems to be their favorite betting round? When do they raise? With what kinds of hands do they usually enter a pot?

3. Low-limit players often are not very adept at reading the strength of their hands compared to the hands of their opponents. Use the information you collected from the above questions to help you *read the cards*.

Get a handle on your own habits—the good, the bad, the beautiful, the ugly—and those of the people you are trying to beat so that it will be easier for you to become a thriver at low-limit poker.

THRIVING

To thrive at the low limits, you must simply outplay most of your opponents most of the time. Learning to do that requires special skills, some of which include:

1. Play fewer hands than you really want to.
2. Make fewer calls than you are inclined to.
3. Read the strength of your opponents' hands more skillfully than they read yours.
4. Play more assertively than you may be accustomed to.
5. Enter games in which there are many players in most pots.
6. Beat the rake by occasionally stealing the blinds.
7. And it doesn't hurt to occasionally get lucky. It feels so good when you win a megapot by combining a favor from capricious Lady Luck with your skill.

To thrive, you must study. Read general poker strategy from the best of the poker gurus, study books on your specialty, and practice before you plunge. You can practice by either dealing and analyzing sample rounds on your kitchen table or by investing in computer software. It also never hurts to have a poker mentor, a guy or gal who is a better player than you are, someone who will spend time discussing winning strategies with you.

WHERE ARE YOU IN YOUR POKER CAREER?

If you've been diving, come in from the pool of losers and advance to the survival stage at the least. Then begin striving to improve your game so that you can become a bona fide poker winner, a thriver. Believe me, there's no other way to go—and it's so much more fun to win than to lose. Wouldn't you agree?

3. WINNING AT TEXAS HOLD'EM

The first time I played Texas hold'em, my ego took a bath and my bankroll took a dive—my chips abandoned me like sailors jumping from a sinking ship. Hold'em was the 747 nonstop to New York for a passenger more accustomed to cruising on the slow boat to China playing seven-card stud and lowball. Fast approaching Tap City, I decided to take a rest stop to study the game more thoroughly before venturing further into its wilderness of position, high kickers and flop hits.

First I bought a book for advanced players, but being a beginner, I got lost in a wilderness of technical concepts that befuddled me. The most important idea that I obtained from the book was its starting hand requirements by position, which I copied on the back of a business card and took to each low-limit session I played.

Next I invested in Tom McEvoy and T.J. Cloutier's *Championship Hold'em*, which has proved to be my most useful resource. The book is written in clear language that makes it easy for new players to understand how to play limit hold'em. I also started practicing my strategy with Wilson Software's *Turbo Texas Hold'em* to get some simulated game experience. I began to survive the rigors of learning this fast, exciting and taxing brand of poker.

Using the experiential mileage under my poker belt and the learning tools I bought like a stock market investor, I've compiled a few strategies for success that will help you to thrive at the myriad low-limit hold'em tables across the nation.

First, let's take a look at the mechanics of the game. If you've never played hold'em, this section is especially for you. But if you already know how the game is played, skip this part and move right along to my ten tips on how to beat low-limit hold'em for big bucks.

HOW TEXAS HOLD'EM IS PLAYED

No other form of poker has captured the imagination of the public like Texas hold'em. Just ask the millions of viewers who watch The World Series of Poker and the World Poker Tour hold'em tournaments on television every week. But as thrilling as it is to see other people push stacks of chips into the center of the table and win big bucks, it's even more exciting when you're the one playing poker's hottest game.

Texas hold'em, which is also commonly referred to as simply **hold'em**, is a form of high poker in which the player with the highest five-card combination at the end of the deal wins the pot, the money that players have wagered and which sits in the middle of the table. The pot is what every player tries to win on each deal.

Each player is dealt two personal cards, called **hole** cards, face down, which he combines with five **community cards**, the **board**, that are dealt face-up in the middle of the table to make his best possible five-card hand.

The best hand in Texas hold'em is a **royal flush**, A-K-Q-J-10 in the same suit. The second-best hand is a **straight flush**, any five cards of the same suit in sequence, such as 10-9-8-7-6 all in hearts, followed by **four of a kind**, four cards of the same rank such as

9-9-9-9. Following these top three hands are a **full house**, three cards of the same rank plus two cards of a second rank; a **flush**, five cards in the same suit; a **straight**, five cards in sequence such as K-Q-J-10-9; **three of a kind**, three cards of the same rank; **two pair**, two groups of cards of equal rank such as J-J and 9-9 (jacks over nines); and **one pair**, one group of equally ranked cards such as K-K.

If nobody holds any of these combinations, then the **high card** of the five best cards will win. The ace is the highest card in hold'em, and the deuce is the lowest. If Player A and Player B have the same high card in their hand, then the next highest card will determine the winner. For example, K-Q-J-8-7 is higher ranked than K-Q-10-8-7. Both players have kings and queens, but the jack is a higher card than the 10 so Player A wins the pot.

To start a round of betting, the dealer gives you and every other player in the game two hole cards face down. When it's your turn to act on the first round of betting, you can do one of three things—fold, call or raise. If you don't like your hole cards, you can **fold** by gently sliding them back to the dealer. Folding indicates that you do not wish to match the bets required and opt out of play. Or you can **call** by matching the size of the required bet, or **raise** by increasing the size of the bet. These latter two actions, calling and raising, keep you active in the hand. If all players fold when a player bets or raises, the remaining player, by default, wins the pot. This can happen at any point during a hold'em hand.

After every player has acted, if at least two players are remaining to contest the pot, the dealer places three community cards face up in the center of the table. This is called the **flop**. Every player who didn't fold before the flop is active and can participate in the betting. The first player to act may either **check**—not wager and pass play on to the next player while still remaining active—or initiate play by betting, placing a wager into the pot. Once any player has bet, then the other active players must either fold, call or raise. If all players check, the betting is closed for the round.

The dealer then deals a fourth community card, called the **turn**, face up in the middle of the table, followed by another round of betting with players having the usual options—checking, betting, raising or folding. Finally, the dealer turns up the fifth and final community card, called the **river**, followed by one last round of betting. Then comes the **showdown**, where the remaining players show their cards and the best hand wins all the money in the pot, or if the pot is tied, then the money is divided evenly.

After a hand is concluded and the winner has claimed the pot—either through other players folding and leaving a default winner, or by having the best hand at the showdown—the dealer reshuffles the cards and deals a new hand.

Texas hold'em is played in two different formats called **cash** or **side** games and **tournament** games. If you are playing in a cash game and lose all your money, you can reach into your pocket for more money and buy additional chips to stay in action. But if you lose all your chips in a tournament, you cannot buy in for any more, that's it, you're done for the day. In this chapter, you will learn how to play cash games. Later, we'll cover how to win tournament games.

Hold'em also is played with two different betting structures. If you are playing **limit hold'em**, the amount of money you can bet at any one time is limited to a prescribed amount. There are all sorts of betting structures, depending upon the amount of money people wish to wager, usually in a two-tier amount such as $4/$8, where the lower tier, the $4 in this example, is the required amount for bets and raises (no more, no less) before the flop and on the flop; and the higher tier, the $8 (again, no more and no less), is the required size of bets and raise on the turn and river. The other betting structure is called **no-limit hold'em**, which is the next poker game I'll cover in this book.

Now let's take a look at how the betting goes. We'll start by reviewing what happens when the cards are first dealt, how you post your blind bets, and then cover how the action proceeds on each betting round.

THE DEAL

Each player is dealt two cards face down, beginning with the player sitting to the left of the **button**. The button is a small disc that indicates who the "dealer" is. It is used by the casino dealer so that he can keep track of who the dealer would be if players dealt the cards themselves, like they used to do in the old days of casino poker and the way people still do in home games. At the start of every new deal, the casino dealer moves the button one seat to the left. When the button has traveled all the way around the table, one **round** of play has been completed.

POSTING THE BLINDS

The first person sitting to the left of the button is called the **small blind** and must post a predetermined bet in front of him before the deal. The second person to the left of the button is called the **big blind**. The big blind must post a prescribed bet before the deal that is double the amount of the small blind.

The purpose of posting blind bets is to stimulate action. That is, the blinds get the pot started so that there will be some money to compete for. Sometimes the blinds force people to play hands that they would not have played if they hadn't already been required to put money into the pot. In cash games, the amount of money that you must post when it's your turn to be the big blind or the small blind remains the same throughout the game.

In limit hold'em, big pairs and high cards rule the roost. Two aces, two kings, two queens, two jacks, and A-K are **premium hands**. You would like to have a pair in your hand and then see one of your rank come on the flop. You also can play other types of hands in different circumstances, but these premium hands are the best ones to play. For example, you also can play suit connecting cards such as Q♥ J♥ or 10♦ 9♦ for profit depending on where you are sitting in relation to the button, called your position at the table. We'll talk more about the importance of position later.

REVIEW OF THE FOUR BETTING ROUNDS

Betting begins after you have been dealt your two **hole** cards (your hand) facedown. The first player who must act is the person who is sitting immediately to the left of the big blind. The action continues clockwise with everyone acting in turn. In the first two rounds only, the big blind is the last player to act. When he has finished acting, the first round of betting is over.

Then the dealer puts three community cards, the **flop**, face-up in the center of the table and the second round of betting begins. This time, the first active player to the left of the button must act first. Then each player who did not fold before the flop can check, bet, call a bet, raise, **reraise** (raise a raise) or fold when it is his turn to act.

After the betting on the flop is finished, the dealer places a fourth community card, called **fourth street** or the **turn**, face-up in the center of the table, followed by another round of betting. Then he deals the final community card, called **fifth street** or the **river**, face-up in the center and there is a final round of betting.

LIMIT TEXAS HOLD'EM BETTING

The number of chips that you can bet in limit hold'em is limited to a fixed upper limit. In a typical $4/$8 limit hold'em game, the blinds are $2/$4 (one-half the amount of the minimum-maximum bets). The maximum amount that you can bet or raise on the first two betting rounds is $4. On the deal (before the flop), the first player to act can either fold by sliding his cards face down toward the dealer; call by placing $4 in chips in the center of the table; or raise by placing $8 in chips in the middle. If someone raises before it is your turn to act, you can fold, call the raise by putting in $8, or reraise to $12. On the flop (the second betting round), the bets are again limited to $4 increments.

The size of the bet doubles on the turn card (the fourth community card) and the river card (the fifth community card). For example, if you are the first player to act on the turn, you must bet $8, no more and no less. If someone bets before it's your turn to act, you can raise to $16, no more and no less. Cardrooms usually allow three or four raises on each round of betting. Once that limit is reached, the betting is **capped**, that is, no more raises are allowed in this betting round.

Because limit hold'em has fixed betting limits, most low-limit hold'em players feel comfortable playing this ever-popular form of hold'em. They know the minimum amount of money it will cost them to play a hand if the pot isn't raised, and can judge whether they want to pay the maximum it will cost to play if the pot is raised. Casinos spread far more limit Texas hold'em games than no-limit hold'em games because they know that players' bankrolls last longer when the betting limits are fixed.

No-limit hold'em is a horse of a different color, a game in which you can lose your entire stake on one hand. Later, I'll give you winning tips on how to beat no-limit games.

When you have mastered selecting the best hands to play, reading the board correctly, understanding the value of your hand, and determining when to hold'em and when to fold'em, you're on your way to beating limit hold'em. Texas hold'em takes only a few hours to learn—but as the old pros say, it takes a lifetime to master the game. Yet even novice players with minimum knowledge and some poker sense are winning money in charity games and casino games across the world. Now let's get on with teaching you how to enjoy yourself to the max by winning at low-limit hold'em.

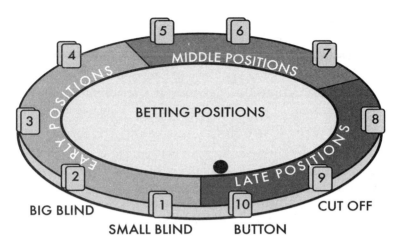

TEN WINNING TIPS

WINNING TIP #1
Your Seat Position Strongly Influences Which Hands You Can Play Profitably

This is the most important concept in low-limit hold'em. The later your position—that is, the closer you are sitting to the button—the more hands you can play and the more aggressive you can be. You can play more aggressively because you have received a lot of information about how the other players intend to play their cards. You have a huge advantage in hold'em when you already know what your opponents are going to do with their hands. When you're sitting very close to the big blind, you're in a front position and can only guess what other players will do after you act. But when you're sitting one or two seats in front of the button, or on the button, you don't need to play the guessing game.

For example, suppose you have a drawing hand such as a Q-J. When you're sitting **up front** (close to the big blind), you have no idea how many players will be entering the pot. The number of players who enter the pot is important to know because unless three or four other people play the hand, you won't have proper pot odds to make it worth your while to play your drawing hand. But if you're sitting one or two seats in front of the button, you will know how many opponents you have and whether the odds will be in your favor. None of this information is available if you are playing from an early position.

"Get it through your head that most hold'em players, even professional players, even world champions, lose vast sums of money from early positions for their entire poker playing careers!" Mike Caro wrote. He believes that a strong argument can be made for playing only aces, kings, and A-K suited when you are sitting in early position in a ten-handed limit hold'em game—especially if aggressive players are still to act after you. Caro is right. If you want to stop losing money in low-limit hold'em, play only your strongest hands in the first or second chair to the left of the big blind.

In a nutshell, tight is right in limit hold'em games, especially when you are sitting in an early position in the betting sequence. Even from middle position you should have a fairly strong starting hand if you are the first or second player to enter the pot. Playing too many hands **out of position** (from a bad position in the betting sequence) is the most common mistake that new players make in limit hold'em games.

WINNING TIP #2
Always Play Good Starting Hands
What is a good Texas hold'em hand? Big cards are what bring home the bacon in hold'em games. As I said earlier, aces, kings, queens, jacks and A-K are the best starting hands, but how about

some others? This is where your position in relation to the big blind and button starts to become more important. You can also play hands such as A-Q, A-J, pocket tens, pocket nines and pocket eights if you are sitting in a middle position and nobody has either entered or raised the pot in front of you. Naturally, the later your position, the better. In fact, in a game with a lot of tight players, you might even raise with these hands if you are sitting in a middle or late position and you are the first player to enter the pot. Why? Because no one sitting in front of you has shown any strength.

But beware! Many hands that contain two face cards are not playable. A lot of otherwise playable hands go way down in value if a tight or solid player raises from an early position. For example, if that little old lady sitting in first position with a layer of dust on her chips suddenly raises, hands like A-Q, A-J and most pocket pairs are simply not playable. You must use good judgment in calling raises, even with strong starting hands.

How about connecting cards such as J-10, 9-8 or 7-6? In low-limit hold'em games, middle and low cards that connect to each other, called **connectors**, can be very profitable hands in multiway pots. But here's the catch—you can play big pairs from any position at the table, but you should play middle or low connectors only from the last two or three positions (on the button or one seat to the right of it). This is good advice because connectors (suited or unsuited) play best in multiway pots, and you only know that the pot will be played multiway after you have found out whether the players sitting in front of you intend to play their hands. To reiterate this important point, you can't know that information if you have to act early in the hand.

WINNING TIP #3
See the Flop as Cheaply as Possible
Unless you have a big pair such as aces, kings or queens, you are usually better off not raising before the flop in low-limit hold'em

games. The reason is simple—lots of players often call raises before the flop in low-limit poker. Whereas big pairs can win the pot without getting any help from the board cards, almost all your other starting hands will need some improvement in order to win. And when you're sitting in one of the front spots (the big blind, the small blind, or the first two seats to the left of the big blind), you'll be out of position on all subsequent action. That is, you will have to act before all or most of your opponents. So, be very careful about entering raised pots from an early table position.

You'll also want to avoid three-way raising action on the flop or turn when you're the "middle man;" that is, you're sitting between the raiser and the reraiser. Of course, the later your position, the more often you can call a raise on any betting round.

I frequently see players **jam the pot** (put in the maximum number of raises) with A-K before the flop, flop nothing but overcards, and still continue to play the hand, often calling raises after the flop. They sometimes even go to the river trying to snag an ace or king. Sometimes they catch it and still lose; other times they miss and complain that the player who called several raises before the flop with 6-5 offsuit, made two pair and beat them. Who played worse, the guy who flopped two pair and then started raising, or the player with the A-K who continued playing after the flop with only overcards?

Cloutier and McEvoy made it clear in *Championship Hold'em* that even if your A-K is suited, it is still a drawing hand, not a made hand such as A-A, K-K, or Q-Q. The big pairs often can win pots without any help from the board cards, but A-K almost always needs a good flop to win the pot. Keep in mind that when you have Big Slick (any A-K), you will only flop a pair to it about 30 percent of the time, and will flop a flush draw only about 11 percent of the time if it is suited.

Do most of your gambling after you see the flop, not before, unless you hold one of the three biggest pairs. That way, you can get away from (fold) your hand cheaply if you don't flop anything good. And if you flop something you like, you can charge your opponents a heavy price to draw against you.

WINNING TIP #4
Learn to Read the Board Cards on Every Street

You must be able to read the board cards correctly throughout the hand. You need to determine the best possible hand on the flop, and the most likely draws that could improve your hole cards or an opponent's cards to the nut hand on fourth street or fifth street. I suggest that you always ask yourself four questions on the flop:

1. What is the best possible hand?
2. Am I holding it or do I have a draw to it?
3. How likely is it that any of my opponents are holding it?
4. What is the probable strength of my opponents' cards?

As each new board card hits the middle of the table, the strength of your hand may change. Therefore you should ask yourself, "At this moment, what is the **nuts**—the best possible hand at the moment?" For example, if you started with two aces in the hole, you had the nuts before the flop. If the flop came A♠ K♣ 9♠, you still have the best possible hand, trip aces. But if the turn card is the J♠, you may not have the nuts any longer. It is possible that an opponent holds a Q-10 and made an ace-high straight on the turn. Another opponent may be holding the 10♠ 8♠ and made a flush on the turn. Either way, your pocket aces are no longer the best hand.

Remember that your best hand can be any combination of none, one, or both of your cards combined with the cards in the middle. Look at it as having a seven-card hand, from which you choose the best five-card combination. If a royal flush is dealt in the community cards, everybody playing the hand has a royal flush because that is the best hand possible. Or if the board cards come with K♠ Q♠ J♠ 10♠ and you have the A♠ in your hand, you have a royal flush and nobody else has one.

If you have two queens in your hand and a queen comes on the board, you have made three queens, called a **set**. If you have the A♣ K♣ and the J♣ 4♣ 8♠ come on the flop, you have the **nut flush draw**. Then if another club comes on the turn or river, you will make the nut flush. You also might flop a pair. Suppose the flop comes K♠ 6♣ 4♣ and you are holding the A♣ K♣. You would have top pair—two kings with an ace kicker—and the nut flush draw, which would make you a very happy camper.

As in all forms of poker, you must be able to make educated guesses as to the strength of your hand compared to the strength of your opponents' hands. You are a detective and the betting actions of your opponents are clues to the probable value of their hands. Try to determine their styles of betting as early as possible by observing them throughout the game, especially when you're not playing in the same hand with them.

For example, does John usually bet a flush draw in late position, but never bets it when he is in the first or second seat after the blinds? Will Howard bet with **rags** (bad cards) on the button if everyone checks? Does Betty play any-ace (an ace with a low kicker)? If Nate checks on the flop but calls your late position bet, ask yourself, "What hand could he be drawing to?" Beware slowplay artists who check-call the flop, check-call the turn, and then check-raise the river—they are usually holding the nut hand or something close to it, and are trying to suck you into their trap.

WINNING TIP #5
Don't Draw to a Lower Hand When a Higher Hand is Possible
When there is a lot of action on the flop and turn, someone usually has either the nut hand or a draw to it. Or they may be play-

ing aggressively to keep you from drawing to a better hand. If you don't have the nuts or a draw to it, why stay in action? That is, why draw to a lesser hand when you know that a higher hand may be likely?

Sometimes they also jam the pot (raise and reraise) to make it expensive for you to draw to a better hand. You must always be careful that the hand you are drawing to will be the best hand if you make it. Suppose you have a flush draw and the board pairs on fourth street. Someone could have made a full house or even four of a kind. This means that even if you make your flush, you will lose. In other words, you are drawing dead. It is very expensive to make your hand only to find that it's a loser. And if the pot is jammed, you probably are a loser for sure.

Some authors contend that in low-limit play, you often have adequate pot odds (because of the frequent multiway action) to justify calling when the board pairs. I'll let you be the judge, but as for me, my P.C. (Poker Conscience) warns that if there has been heavy betting action, my flush draw usually is toast.

In *Championship Hold'em*, Cloutier mentions that another risky draw is "continuing [calling bets] in a raised pot when all you have is two overcards to the flop." Again, he's talking about those optimistic losers who chase pots with A-K when they have no draws other than catching either an ace or a king on the turn or river.

Other sage advice is not to draw to a straight when a flush is possible—and don't draw to the low end of a straight when a higher straight can be made. Poker aficionados call it "drawing to the idiot end of the straight," and you'll find out why after you've made a fool of yourself a few times losing to the higher hand. For example suppose you limped into the pot in late position with the 7-6 of spades. The flop comes 9-8-7 **rainbow** (three different suits). You have made a pair with a draw to a straight. Take another look at that board. What if a 10 comes off the deck on fourth street? Aha!

You have made your straight, but anyone who has a jack has made a bigger straight. You may have only three outs—the remaining three jacks in the deck—just to get a tie. Even if you stay in the pot and hit a jack, you might then find a player with a queen in his hand!—and you still lose.

WINNING TIP #6
Play More Conservatively in Games With a Low Bring-in Bet, Most Jackpot Games, and Kill-Pot Games

In some $4/$8 hold'em games, the small blind is $1, the big blind is $2, and the preflop come-in bet is $2. With a $4 maximum wager on the flop and the $2 come-in bet at half that amount, these games have a low bring-in bet in relation to the maximum bet on the flop. Because it is so cheap to see the flop, many low-limit players will enter more pots than they would if the bring-in bet were $4 (a full bet on the flop instead of a half-bet).

The better strategy is to enter fewer pots, which means that you will be playing somewhat tighter than most of your opponents. Don't use the lower bring-in bet as an excuse to play more hands. Some players will lower their starting requirements too much and start gambling with speculative hands more often than they should. This leads to financial loss. When you start playing too many hands, you have lowered your game to their level. Don't do it, not once, not ever.

"I don't look at what the purse is or the prize money. You play. And when you play, you play to win, period."

Tiger Woods

Now to my favorite saw, the jackpot games. In addition to the usual **rake**—the amount the casino takes from the pot to pay for their services—a jackpot contribution is taken from every pot in "jackpot poker." If you enter more pots than optimal strategy calls for, your stack is paying for both of these extractions.

Don't allow a mediocre jackpot to lure you into playing looser than you should. Although I have seen many hold'em players call double-raised pots with low pairs from a front position—hoping to crack the jackpot with quads beaten by quads—I strongly advise that you do not *unless* the jackpot is huge. In that case, Tom McEvoy suggests that you might see more flops than you ordinarily would because of the overlay (the superior odds) the jackpot is giving you to play.

Small pairs and suited connectors are the favorite starting hands of many jackpot players because winning the jackpot usually requires either aces-full or four-of-a-kind (or better) to be beaten by a better hand. If you do decide to play in a jackpot game, be sure you understand all the rules and how much additional rake the casino is going to charge you. For an in-depth discussion of jackpot strategy in hold'em games, I suggest that you read the excellent chapter on how to play jackpot games in *Championship Hold'em*.

Another type of game in which you might consider playing tighter is low-limit hold'em games that have a kill. Two types of kill-pot games are played in casinos, full-kill games and half-kill games. In a $4/$8 hold'em game with a **full-kill**, the limits for the next hand dealt are doubled under certain circumstances. In a game with a **half-kill**, the limits are increased by 50 percent. Each cardroom has its own rules for determining when a kill pot is declared. In some casinos, the kill goes into effect on the next hand after a player has won two pots in a row. In other casinos, the kill is activated on the next hand after a player wins a pot that exceeds a certain amount of money. In either situation, the kill is in effect for that hand only—unless the same player wins again. In that case, the limits remain at the higher level until the "killer" loses a pot.

A disc with the word "kill" printed on it is placed in front of the player who either (a) won two pots in a row, or (b) won a big pot ($80, for example). If you are the designated killer, you must place a forced bet in front of the kill button that is equal to the big blind at the new, higher limits. In a full-kill $4/$8 game, the limits rise to $8/$16 for the next hand; and in a half-kill game, the limits rise to $6/$12.

Is it our greedy nature or just circumstance that when a kill-pot is being played, it seems that more players enter the pot? Or could it be the contagious excitement that comes from playing a hand at limits that are higher than we usually would play? I don't have the answer to my own rhetorical questions, but I do have the answer to avoiding the agony of defeat while enjoying the thrill of playing at a higher limit: Only play your best hands. Don't get sucked into the action and you won't get sucked out on when you miss your draws.

WINNING TIP #7
Bluffing is Overrated in Limit Hold'em

People get the idea that the bluff is a big part of limit hold'em because they've seen players bluff in no-limit hold'em tournaments on television. Bluffs may be exciting to watch, but they work far better in no-limit hold'em games than they do in limit hold'em games. This is especially true in low-limit games.

Limit hold'em games are designed to have a showdown on the river. The pot is often so large that players with very marginal hands will call. They only have to call a single bet to try to win a pot that may already contain 15 or more bets. Also, a "sheriff" usually is sitting at the table. The sheriff is a player who keeps everybody honest by calling suspected bluffs and won't be able to sleep at night if he thinks he has been bluffed. These are two reasons why bluffing too often is a mistake in low-limit hold'em games.

Heed the advice that tournament champions Cloutier and McEvoy: "All forms of limit poker are designed to have a showdown. Players frequently bluff in big-bet poker, in pot-limit and no-limit games. But remember that in limit games, the pot may have 20 bets in it and it is only going to cost an opponent one more bet to call. Players are going to make that call most of the time if they have any kind of hand at all. Therefore you simply cannot steal many pots by bluffing in limit hold'em."

To put it another way, you simply cannot win by bluffing at a multiway pot. Why? Because in hotly contested pots with three, four or five players, your opponents will seldom fold at the river because it usually costs them only one bet to call. And oftentimes there will be more than one caller at the showdown. After all, if the pot is multiway and several players have stayed to the river, they must have some sort of hand, right?

Here's another way to think about a multiway pot: When several players already have invested lots of bets, the pot becomes what we call a "protected pot." A single bet at the river will never induce anyone with even a remote chance of winning to fold for that final bet because the pot is "protected" from theft by its grandiose size. Even players with the second-best and third-best hands usually will call. Therefore you simply must have the best hand to win a multiway pot at the river—or at least a better hand than anyone else has. But for sure, you cannot steal a protected pot with a bluff-bet.

When can you bluff? The three game conditions you are looking for when you attempt a bluff are:

1. When the pot is small;
2. When you have superior position over your opponents (you're the button);

3. When you are playing against only one or two opponents who play on the conservative side (which seldom is the case in low-limit games).

WINNING TIP #8
Kickers are Very Important in Hold'em

When you have been dealt non-paired cards such as A-K, Q-J, or A-5, the second-highest card in your hand is called the **kicker**. The higher the kicker, the higher the value of your hand. That's why you would prefer playing an A-K than an A-Q, and you would rather play a Q-J than a Q-10. At the showdown, if you and your opponent both have aces, the player with the higher kicker will win the pot. Read the following true story to see how it works.

I was teaching a close personal friend of mine the basics of how to play hold'em. An expert bridge player, she caught on quickly, so we went to one of my old hunting grounds in Vegas to practice playing some $2/$4 hold'em for real money against real people, rather than the imaginary opponents we'd been practicing against on the kitchen table.

After a few hands had been dealt, Jo entered a pot from second position. I felt certain that she had a good hand, probably a big pair or at least an A-J. The flop came A-4-6 and she bet $2. Three players called. The turn was a queen. She bet $4 and only the player on the button called. When the river showed a 5, she checked and so did her opponent. She turned over A-7 offsuit and he showed A-10 suited. Her best hand was A-Q-7-6-5. His best hand was A-Q-10-7-6, with which he won the pot.

"Oops!" I thought. "I might not have emphasized the importance of having a big kicker in hold'em." Sure enough, she said she figured she had the best hand until the river when it looked like a straight was possible. The lesson: Be very conscious of your kicker in low-limit hold'em.

Here's another thing to consider when you play two high cards. If you decide to play a connecting hand such as Q-10 from a late position, you would far rather see a 10 come on the flop than a queen. Why? Because there are three kickers that can beat your queen if a queen comes on the board—ace, king and jack. Looking at it from that viewpoint, your queen doesn't have a very good kicker, does it? Furthermore, A-Q, K-Q, and Q-J are the types of hands that people play in low-limit hold'em from just about any position. Your 10, however, has a pretty good kicker in the queen. A lot of low-limit players like to play hands such as J-10, 10-9 and even 10-8 suited. The point is that when you do not have a strong kicker, you would rather see the *lower* of your two hole cards appear on the board.

You hear so much about players having "kicker trouble" when they play hands with an ace and a small card (A-6, A-8, A-9), and rightfully so. Just be aware that in low-limit hold'em, people love to play **any-ace** hands—that is, an ace with any other card. Any-ace hands look like the U.S. mint in Denver to them, particularly if the ace is suited to its inferior partner. This is why, when you play a beautiful hand like pocket kings, you should be afraid—very afraid—if an ace comes on the flop. Proceed with caution and you won't get many speeding tickets in low-limit hold'em.

WINNING TIP #9
Psychology Plays a Minor Role in Low-limit Poker
Psychology has been glamorized by those swift mental ploys you see players using in big televised tournaments. Of course, the commentator adeptly points out what Boston Billy is doing when he puts a psychological hammerlock on Lost Louie. "Aha! So that's what happening," I sometimes say to myself, not wanting my mate to know that I didn't understand what the heck Billy was up to.

Solid basic strategy is far more important in low-limit hold'em than trying to get tells on your opponents, or using sophisticated psychological ploys to outfox them. Basically, so few players are paying close attention in the small games that you probably will be wasting your time and effort trying to out-psych players who do not yet have enough experience to appreciate or respond correctly to your coolest moves.

Knowing some simple mathematical concepts—such as your number of outs that will improve your hand—is essential. In *The Sky's The Limit*, high-stakes player Doug Young points out that, "When you're playing the lower limits, you cannot survive without knowing and using math to your advantage. In the small games, math is what it's all about."

Although psychology is a component of low-limit play, it is not nearly as crucial to your success as it is at high-limit poker. Playing good basic strategy and knowing the starting hands to play from different positions at the table is far more important than trying to psyche out your opponents. You don't have to be a rocket scientist or a math genius to be successful. Come to think of it, the only time I ever played with a rocket scientist at the poker table, I found that he was a duck out of water. If your opponent doesn't know the relative strength of either his hand or your hand, fancy plays and psychological ploys will be wasted on him. Many novice low-limit hold'em players have a very simple philosophy—when in doubt, call!

WINNING TIP #10
Maintain Your Discipline
In low-limit Texas hold'em games, maintaining your discipline is the key to success. Avoiding the *tilt factor* will assist you in overcoming short-term bad luck, while helping ensure long-term success. What exactly is the tilt factor? Going on *tilt* means that after a series of **bad beats** (big losses, usually when a strong hand loses to an even stronger one) an otherwise solid player suddenly starts playing a lot more hands—usually marginal ones and often out

of position. He lowers his starting hand requirements and starts chasing his losses.

Sometimes even top professional players go on tilt. When that happens, a game that would not be considered a playable game by most standards suddenly becomes a thing of beauty. The best pros know enough about discipline and their own tilt factor to get up from the table and take a walk when things start to go bad. I would advise you to do the same. I don't know of a player on the planet who, after suffering two or three bad beats in a row, can honestly say that he is not somewhat emotionally upset over the way things are going.

Controlling our emotions is the key to success. How can we dominate our opponents if we are not in control of ourselves?

A WORD FROM P.C.

"Aren't you grinding your 'jackpot poker' axe a bit too sharply, Shane? After all, you *did* win a hold'em jackpot when you were just beginning to play the game," my Poker Conscience chides me.

"Listen, P.C., that's confidential information. I didn't even know there was a jackpot back in '87 at the Commerce Casino when I beat out those aces full of kings with quad aces playing my A-10 offsuit from first position (certainly a faux pas, I freely admit, but I was a bona fide rookie back them). Besides, I only got the small end of it (about $1,200) and I haven't hit one since. It was just a lucky fluke."

With that, P.C. retreats, probably because he (she? it?) knows that these success tips can shorten your trip from simply surviving to continually thriving on your poker journey to ultimate success and enjoyment at low-limit hold'em. Bon voyage!

4. LIMIT HOLD'EM PRACTICE HANDS

The practice hands presented in this chapter are adapted from *Beat Texas Hold'em*, the book that Tom McEvoy and I wrote a few years ago for beginning players. I know you'll find them helpful in learning some of the nuances of playing special types of hands in limit hold'em.

1. BIG PAIRS (A-A AND K-K)

Suppose you're **under the gun** (the first seat to the left of the big blind) in a cash game or tournament and you look down at the boss hand, **two aces**. It doesn't matter how many chips you have in front of you or what stage of the tournament you're playing; bring the pot in for a raise. Don't **limp** (just call) with two aces unless there is a maniac sitting behind you who raises every pot. In that case, since you know that he's going to raise the pot anyway, you might just call and then reraise if he raises.

Whether you're in first position, middle position or last position, raise with this hand. Why? To limit the field. You don't mind playing aces against one or two players, but you don't want to be forced to play against everybody at the table. A pair of aces is the best hand that you can start with in limit hold'em and you want to win the pot with without giving your opponents a free ride to beat you with inferior hands. If the opponents who called your bet or raise before the flop are reasonable players, lead at it on the flop unless big connected cards flop. A dangerous flop to your pair of aces is any three big connected cards.

Play **pocket kings** about the same way you play pocket aces. Just be aware that if an ace hits the board on the flop, you have to back off. Suppose someone sitting in an early position has raised the pot and another player has called the raise before the flop. Reraise with your two kings. Make them pay to get a chance at catching a good flop with a weak ace, for example. Of course, there are some inexperienced limit hold'em players who never lay down an "ace-anything" hand before the flop, but even though you might lose to them now and then, these are the kinds of players that you want to play against because you will beat them in the long run.

Try to get it heads-up with your pocket "cowboys." If you put in raise number two and your opponent puts in raise number three, you have to call him. There's a chance that you might be up against aces, but it's a small chance. Watch your opponents. How aggressively do they play two jacks or small pairs? Do they put in a third bet with two queens? Let that information guide in your betting decisions.

In summary, play two kings very aggressively before the flop and hope that an ace doesn't hit the board. Remember that when you're playing against only one or two players, a big pair has a good chance of holding up, but if you're playing against a lot of players, you can't be nearly as aggressive with it. This is why you always raise with your kings to try to play the hand heads-up.

After the flop you have to play pocket kings according to which cards come on the board. You face the same types of danger flops with pocket kings that you face with pocket aces, only more so because of the danger of an ace flopping. You're starting with the second-best hand in hold'em, but when you have kings, it sometimes seems like all the other cards in the deck are aces!

2. BIG PAIRS (Q-Q AND J-J)

Pocket queens is a raising hand before the flop from any position in limit hold'em. And sometimes it is a raising hand. Always keep in mind that there are two overcards to the queen that people play all the time in limit hold'em. For example, suppose a solid player in seat one raises before the flop and another good player calls the raise before it gets to you. One or the other of them might have two aces, two kings, or an A-K. For that reason, just call with your pocket queens, don't reraise.

Now let's say that a player in the first seat next to the big blind has raised and a solid player in the second seat has reraised. You're sitting in the third seat with six players (including the two blinds) waiting to act after you. What do you do? Usually, you fold. Although you've picked up a strong hand, you don't have any money involved in the pot, and since it's been raised and reraised before you've even had a chance to act, it's easy to just throw them away. So what if the guy in the first seat only has two tens? The player next to him might have two aces or two kings or A-K. Why take a chance of losing money against such heavy betting when you can get a new hand to play in about two minutes?

Pocket jacks is a hand that you can play from any position at the table when you are the *first* player to enter the pot. If you get reraised, just call. After you see the flop, you can decide whether to continue with the hand. Now suppose you're in late position and a couple of players have limped in front of you. You still raise the pot. Why? To try to get everyone sitting behind you, including the blinds, to fold. Another reason is to build the pot. The factor that determines the value of your pocket jacks is the number of people playing the hand with you. The more players in the pot, the more vulnerable you are. Heads-up, two jacks is a big, big hand.

If you're sitting one seat in front of the button (the **cutoff seat**) or on the button, raise with pocket jacks if the pot hasn't been raised yet. Your raise might knock out the people between you and the first bettor. If someone reraises, just flat-call. If you get unlucky and an ace, king or queen flops, you can always fold the hand. But if the flop comes with a jack in it, bingo! But when it comes with overcards and you have two or more opponents, there's a pretty good chance that you're beaten, so you say adios to your "hooks" and send them into the muck if anyone bets.

3. BIG CONNECTING CARDS (A-K AND A-Q)

In any position other than the small or big blind, you can reraise with **A-K**. And if you've been watching your opponents, you might even *reraise* against most of them. You can raise from the blinds but usually, do not reraise because you will have to act first from the flop on, which puts you out of position.

 If you're sitting in a late position and somebody has raised in front of you, reraise with an A-K. You will have them on the defensive because they will have to act first after the flop. If you're in the first three positions, bring it in for a raise. If you're in fourth, fifth, six or seventh position, you can reraise with A-K. And again, if you're in the small or big blind, the most you should do is raise with the hand, you should not reraise with it.

Many of today's limit hold'em players play A-K, or ace-anything in fact, like it's the total nuts. A lot of players raise with A-Q, A-J, A-10 and even A-9 because they love playing any suited ace. You're a big favorite over these types of hands when you have an A-K—and that is why you always reraise with it if anyone raises in front of you, meaning that you will not have to act first after the flop. You might lose a few pots against opponents with weaker aces, but in the long run you're going to win a lot more often than you lose because you started with the best hand.

An A-Q is a good hand in limit hold'em because so many people these days are playing small connectors and lesser holdings that are not as strong as an A-Q. You can raise with A-Q from any position to try to limit the field, just as you do with A-K, but don't usually reraise with it. If the flop comes ace-high or queen-high, you have a pretty good hand. When the flop comes queen high, you have top pair-top kicker; and when it comes ace-high, you have top pair with second-best kicker. You would like to be up against a K-Q or Q-J when the flop comes queen-high because then you're sitting in clover with a better kicker.

There are a few situations in a tournament, however, when you might reraise with an A-Q. Suppose you're sitting on the button and a player who has only enough chips for one more bet raises the pot. In this case, reraise to put him all in. By raising him all-in, you're not going to get blown out on the flop if it doesn't come with anything that helps you—and hopefully, you will knock him out of action.

Another situation where you can reraise with A-Q is when you're in very late position and an aggressive player sitting to your immediate right raises. You reraise in this spot because you probably have the best hand, plus you will get to act after he acts on the flop.

4. MEDIUM CONNECTORS (J-10 AND 8-7)

You don't want to give a **J-10** too much credit because it has definite liabilities. You can play it, of course, but J-10 is a hand that you must play very carefully under the right conditions. Some of the right conditions include when you are in a late position in a multiway, unraised pot, and when you are defending the big blind for a single bet.

In a raised pot, you usually fold with J-10. A lot of players who believe that J-10 is a super hand, suited or unsuited, forget that even a lowly Q-6 offsuit has a higher card in it than a J-10. And if you flop either a jack or a 10 as top pair, you don't have a good kicker, do you?

If the pot has been raised and called before it gets to you, you are a definite underdog in the hand with only a J-10, suited or unsuited. Being suited does not increase its value enough to justify calling a raise. Even if the pot is raised and nobody else calls between you and the raiser, your J-10 is still a dog.

The real strength of J-10 is the 10. A straight cannot be made without a 10 or a 5, so the power of J-10 is the multitude of straights that you can make with it. You can flop a lot of different made straights to this hand, and you can flop a lot of straight draws with it.

In tournaments, J-10 is the type of hand that can cost you all of your money. Suppose you call a bet before the flop and you flop some possibilities. You call another bet on the flop, and you don't make your draw on fourth street. Now you have to decide whether to continue. You might think, "I've already lost two bets before the flop and a bet on the flop. Now it's going to cost me a double bet on the turn. But I've got so much money in the pot already, I'm gonna continue." That's the dilemma that hands like J-10 can put you in. Take your loss and move on to the next hand.

Hands such as **8-7 suited** are virtually unplayable in early to middle position. If you're in late position and a few limpers are in the pot, that's a different story—now you have position. You need to have at least two callers in front of you to play the hand, even when you're next to the button or on the button.

You have to get a perfect flop to a hand that's only 8-high, otherwise you can lose a lot of chips. For that reason, it just isn't a hand that you usually want to play in a tournament. The hands that you really want to play in tournament poker are the ones that you *don't* have to get a perfect flop to—and that's one of the big differences between tournament play and cash-game play.

5. MEDIUM PAIRS (10-10 AND 9-9)

Pocket tens is a very playable hand in a lot of limit hold'em situations—but it isn't playable at all in other situations. For example, you usually should pass if solid players sitting in early positions have bet, raised and reraised before the flop. However, if everybody else comes into the pot and you are getting a huge price for calling the double or triple bet, you might call. Just keep in mind that you probably need to flop a set to stay in the hand. With two tens, you're the "favorite" to see one or more overcards hit the board

Pocket tens have the best chance of holding up against one or two opponents. If the pot is played multiway, you almost always have to flop a set or make a lucky straight on the turn or river to win the pot. In fact the only advantage that two tens have over some of the other pairs is a 10 (or a 5) is always necessary to make a straight.

If you are in early position, you usually can bring it in for a raise. When you are in middle position and three or four people have passed in front of you, automatically raise. If one or two players have limped into the pot, usually just flat-call to try to see the flop cheaply. If you are playing in a super loose game where everybody is playing a lot of hands, you might want to just call with pocket tens from early position to mix up your play a little bit in the hope of flopping a set. You limp in because you are expecting to get multiway action, and because players at these loose tables don't usually respect early-position raises.

If you are sitting in a late position and someone who is sitting to your right in middle to late position brings it in for a raise, you generally want to reraise to try to isolate and get the action heads up. Your equity goes up if you can drive everybody else out of the pot, you probably have the best starting hand, and you will have position on the raiser. If he reraises, just flat-call and make a decision after you see the flop. Obviously, if you flop a 10 you have a powerful hand. Your main concern then becomes deciding how to extract the most money you can from your opponent. Usually, the later the position that the initial raise comes from, the less strength the raiser needs to bring it in for a raise.

Pocket nines can be a very tricky hand to play. It's a little too good to throw away, but it's also very vulnerable in an early position. Nines, tens and jacks are in about the same category. A pair of jacks is about 50-50 to catch one or more overcards on the flop, and a pair of nines is weaker of course. In early position you might just limp in with pocket nines because you want to see the flop cheaply.

Suppose you're on the button with pocket nines and one or two people have limped into the pot. You usually would just call because if you raise, the limpers probably are going to call the single raise—and the types of hands that they often limp with are the connecting cards such as Q-J or J-10, overcards to your nines.

But you might also raise. Raising will cost you only one extra bet, you know that most or all the limpers are going to call you, and your raise will build the pot. You're hoping to flop a set and win a decent pot with the nines, realizing that you can fold them if overcards hit the board on the flop. If just one overcard hits the board and everybody checks, you can bet. But what if the flop comes with two overcards? In that case, the limpers often will check to the raiser, thus giving you a chance at a free card by also checking.

A big mistake that people make in hold'em is betting after all their opponents have checked to them when the flop comes with two or more overcards. Why not take the free card? If you bet and someone check-raises, you will have to fold the hand immediately and will wind up losing a bet when it didn't have to cost you anything to see one more card.

6. SMALL PAIRS (8-8 AND LOWER)

Pocket eights or sevens usually are not hands that you want to play unless the pot will be played with a big field, in which case you don't mind gambling with the small pairs in the hope of flopping a set. Naturally this means that you are sitting in a late table position, because otherwise you cannot be sure that the pot will be played multiway. In other words, you can play small pairs from late position for the minimum bet when there are several callers in front of you.

What should you do if you limp into the pot with a small pair and someone raises behind you? You can call one more bet, but if an opponent raises behind you and another player reraises, the proper play usually is to fold. If you are playing against conservative players and no one has entered the pot, you can even raise from late position with a small pocket pair. Just remember that you must be the first player to enter the pot with only one or two players who can act after you bet. Don't try this play if most of your opponents are loose players because they usually will call you with any ace or any suited high card-low card combination.

Although a **pair of fives** is a small pair, it has an added value: A 5 or a 10 is always needed to make a straight. If you catch a flop such as 4-3-2 (which gives you an open-end straight draw and an overpair), you're in clover. If you're lucky enough to catch an ace on the board, and one of your opponents is holding an ace, you've beaten him with your straight. Of course it's a little bit dangerous if a 5 hits on the turn to give you a set because, unfortunately, the player with the ace has made the straight! You don't necessarily have to fold in this scenario, just play the hand cautiously.

Always keep in mind that limit hold'em is a big-card game. If you play small pairs from an early position, you always take the risk of losing your money. You must hit a set or get some other fantastic flop to win with these little pairs. (Sets will win 80 percent or more of the time when you flop one.)

The best strategy for playing sixes or lower when you are dealt them in the first three or four seats is to throw them away, especially in a tournament. People play a lot more hands in cash games because the pots are multiway far more often than they are in tournaments, and they play a lot of small pairs in the hope of flopping a set and winning a monster pot. There's nothing wrong with that, but don't do it in a tournament because small pairs usually will just burn up your money.

7. SMALL CONNECTORS (5-4)

The higher your connectors, the better off you are. **Small suited connectors**, of course, are not as strong as the middle suited connectors because many times they make the weak end of the straight. If you have a 5-4 suited, the only time that you can make the nut straight is when A-2-3, 2-3-6, or 3-6-7 are on the board. If the flop comes 8-7-6 you can be in a world of hurt with the "idiot" end of the straight.

A flush is not what you are hoping to make if your small connectors are suited. For example, suppose you flop a flush. Any player who has a single higher card in your suit can make a bigger flush on the turn or river if a fourth suited card hits the board, and most of them will call on the flop to see fourth street. If the fourth flush card comes on fourth street, you have to be very careful in deciding whether you wish to continue with the hand.

You can play this type of hand when you are in the small blind and it costs you only one-half a bet more to see the flop. You also might defend the big blind with small connectors in a multiway pot. Or you may play it for a single bet on the button when at least two other people already are in the pot and you don't think that either of the blinds will raise.

8. ANY-ACE SUITED

In loose cash games you'll see a lot of people playing **any-ace hands**, particularly if the ace is suited. These types of players play very aggressively, usually overbetting their hands and giving a lot of loose action.

Any-ace suited is a weak hand, although there are a few situations in which you might play it. For example, you can call with any-ace from the small blind for half a bet if the pot has not been raised. You also might call with this type of hand when you're on or next to the button in an unraised pot and several players already are in the pot. In this case you figure that the ace might be good because if someone else had a big ace, he probably would have raised. And if everyone passed to you on the button, you can raise with an any-ace hand to attack the blinds.

Just remember that if several people have limped into the pot and you call on the button with a hand such as the A♠ 6♠, you're not looking to win with a lone ace. If you happen to win with the ace by itself, lucky you—but what you're really hoping for on the flop is two sixes, an ace and a 6, or three spades.

9. ONE-GAP HANDS (Q-10)

Connected cards that are not connected to the next-lowest card are called **one-gap** hands, **two-gap** hands, or **three-gap** hands depending on the number of missing ranks between the high card and the low card. Q-10 is a one-gap hand that people frequently play in low-limit hold'em games. Being suited always makes a hand more valuable, but whether suited or unsuited, Q-10 is a hand that requires a lot of skill to play properly, especially in tournaments. It is what we call a **trouble hand**, one that you can play primarily from a late table position when the pot has not been raised.

From early position, fold this trouble hand. If you just call from an early position and an opponent reraises, the hand goes way down in value, which is one reason why Q-10 is awkward to play in the first three seats to the left of the big blind. For example, suppose you call with Q-10, the action is raised behind you, and you call the raise. If you flop a pair to the hand, you cannot know for certain whether you have the best kicker. Many people play Q-Q, Q-J, K-Q, A-Q, so when you flop a queen to your Q-10, you're likely to have a big kicker problem. And you're out of position in the betting sequence since you will have to make a betting decision before the players who are sitting behind you.

If you are sitting in the cutoff seat (one place to the right of the button) or on the button, you might call from late position with Q-10, but you generally would not raise with it. However if nobody else has entered the pot, you might raise with Q-10 to try to get heads-up with the blinds.

Q-10 is an especially troublesome hand. Suppose the flop comes with Q-J-4, which is an extremely dangerous board when you have a Q-10. Although you have flopped top pair, you have a weak kicker. And if you hit a 10 on the turn to make two pair, the 10 would make a straight for anyone who has an A-K or a K-9. Furthermore, someone may already have queens and jacks or even a set of fours. You may even get a good flop for your hand and still have to fold it. Suppose the flop comes Q-9-7. If someone bets and another player raises before it's your turn to act, you must fold because the chances are slim to zero that you have the best hand.

So what kind of flop do you want? You'd much rather see a 10 on the flop than a queen because your queen would be a decent kicker for the 10. What you're really hoping to make is two pair, trips, or a lucky straight. Therefore your ideal flops would be Q-10-2, 10-10-3, or A-K-J.

10. TWO-GAP HANDS (K-10)

With this two-gapper, in which you're missing the Q-J, you have to be very careful to select just the right circumstances in which you play your **K-10**. For example, in a limit hold'em tournament, you might play K-10 when you are in late position and nobody else has entered the pot. In this situation K-10 is a reasonable hand with which to attack the blinds by raising, but only if they are conservative players who are likely to fold against your raise. And in a cash game you can call when you are sitting on the button and one or more players have already entered the pot for the minimum bet.

Be forewarned, however, that this two-gap hand can spell trouble any time that you play it in a raised pot. Against a solid player who raises from up front, fold a K-10 even if you are in the big blind and no one else has called the raise. If several people have called the raise, you might consider playing the hand if it is suited. Ask yourself, "If Solid Sam has raised from early position and several people have called him, what could they be calling with?" They could easily be holding K-Q, A-10, K-J, or better. In that case, if you don't catch a lucky straight or two pair to your K-10, you probably are beaten.

Now suppose you are in the big blind with a K-10 and an action player raises from the button. In this situation, you can call the extra bet to see the flop. And if you are the small blind and only one other player has entered the pot for the minimum bet, you can call for one-half a bet to see what comes on the flop. What if you have K-10 in the small blind and nobody else is in the pot, meaning that you can play the hand head-up against the big blind? In this scenario, you can raise with K-10 to try to win the blinds.

Always remember that K-10 has more value if the pot has not been raised. What do people normally raise with? Big pairs and high cards with big kickers. That is why you play K-10 only when you are sitting in a late position and the pot has not been raised. Because people limp in with hands such as K-Q, K-J and A-10, you still have to be cautious even if you flop top pair. Suppose the flop comes K-8-4. If someone bets from early position into a field of four or five people, you don't like your pair of kings a whole lot because there's a good chance that the bettor has a higher kicker. You would much rather see a flop such as 10-5-2 because your king is the second-best kicker possible. You just hope that nobody has an A-10!

5. WINNING AT NO-LIMIT TEXAS HOLD'EM

If you've never played no-limit Texas hold'em, poker's most exciting game, buckle up! You're in for the ride of your life with the "Cadillac of poker," the nickname that Doyle Brunson, the world's most famous poker player and the author of *Super System*, gave it.

In limit hold'em, the amount of money you can bet at any one time is limited to a prescribed amount. But if you are playing no-limit hold'em, your bet is limited only by the amount of money you have in front of you—and you can bet it all at one time if you want to.

At one time, it would've been difficult to find a cardroom that spread any no-limit hold'em games. Today it is not uncommon for cardrooms to have several no-limit hold'em games in action, usually ranging from $1/$2 blinds and $2/$5 blinds, with some games as high as $5/$10 blinds. A $5/$10 no-limit hold'em game is far bigger than a $5/$10 limit hold'em game because players can bet as much as they want of the chips in front of them.

The popularity of no-limit hold'em took a major leap in 2003 when an amateur player who had never before played no-limit

Don Gay

"You can't let the bull read your resume."

World Champion Bull Rider

hold'em in a casino won the championship of poker and $2.5 million at the World Series of Poker. Appropriately, his name is Chris Moneymaker. Many seasoned veterans in the poker world pay tribute to Moneymaker as the main force behind the explosion in the popularity of poker in recent years. After all, if someone with so little casino poker experience could win that much money, television audiences figure they could too. With that in mind, let's start learning how to take the baby steps that will rapidly lead you up the ladder of success in no-limit hold'em poker.

NO-LIMIT TEXAS HOLD'EM BETTING

No-limit hold'em is the poker game that you most often see being played on television tournaments. Basically, the game is set up in the same way as limit hold'em with one major exception that sets it apart from its more conservative cousin: You can bet any amount at any time up to the amount of chips you have.

Suppose the size of the small blind is $1,000 and the big blind is $2,000 at the championship table of a World Poker Tour tournament you're watching on television. The dealer has just dealt two cards to each player. He has not dealt any community cards yet. The player sitting to the immediate left of the big blind is the first person to act. He has to match the size of the big blind (call) if he wants to play his cards. In this example, $2,000 is the least that he can bet in order to play the hand.

If he wants to raise, he must bet at least double the amount of the big blind, $4,000. But if he wants to, he can raise any amount up to the number of chips he has in his stack. For example, if he has

$80,000 in front of him, he can raise to $30,000 by announcing, "Raise to $30,000" or pushing the equivalent number of chips in front of him. Or he can bet his entire $80,000 by announcing, "All in."

In no-limit hold'em, you can bet all your chips on any of the four betting rounds. If you want to bet all your chips at once, you simply announce, "I'm going all in!" and push all your chips into the center of the table. An opponent can call your all-in bet even if he doesn't have as many chips as you have bet. In that case, the size of the bet can be no bigger than the smaller stack. If you have the larger stack and lose the hand, you get to keep the remaining chips in your stack.

For example, suppose you have $6,000 in chips and go all in against Player B, who has a total of $4,000 in chips. Alas, Player B wins the pot at the showdown. But the good news is that he is eligible to win only an amount that is equal to his chip stack. Therefore you get a refund of $2,000 in chips because Player B could only call $4,000 of your original bet.

A player who does not have enough chips to call the minimum bet can still play the hand by putting in all the chips he has left. For instance, if he only has $3,000 in chips when the big blind is $4,000, he can call with everything he has by announcing that he is all in.

Here's the risky part of playing no-limit hold'em—you can lose all your money on a single bet. It takes a different breed of cat to be willing to take that big a risk, but it sure makes the game exciting to watch on television!

Of course, no-limit hold'em is played primarily in tournament mode on TV, which also adds to its glamour. If a player loses all of his chips in a *cash* game, he can reach into his pocket and put more money on the table. But if he loses all his chips in a tournament game, he is out of action and must head for the **rail** (the barrier that is placed between players and spectators). Nobody who plays serious poker likes being on the rail.

HOW MUCH SHOULD YOU BET IN NO-LIMIT HOLD'EM?

You don't have to decide how much you should bet in limit hold'em, you only need to know how much you can bet. Most limit-hold'em players who decide to give no-limit hold'em a shot have to move outside their comfort zones and learn new betting skills. Deciding how much to bet or raise can pose quite a problem for new players.

Watching televised tournaments, it is sometimes hard to understand why players bet as many or as few chips as they do, but the truth is that most no-limit hold'em players follow a few simple guidelines that help them determine how much to bet. As a general rule, when you are the first person to enter the pot, you should raise three to four times the size of the big blind. Sometimes you might just call the minimum bet, and sometimes you might bet five or six times the size of the big blind. In special circumstances you might even bet all of your chips (move all in). You'll learn more about betting, along with other key concepts, in the following winning tips for no-limit hold'em, contributed by Tom McEvoy, former World Champion of Poker champion.

TEN WINNING TIPS

WINNING TIP #1
Big Pairs and High Cards are the Boss Hands in No-limit Hold'em
No-limit hold'em is a game of big cards. Playing small pairs and medium suited connectors—unless you can play them cheaply from late position—is simply too expensive. The five best starting hands are aces, kings, queens, A-K and jacks. You usually can

play these hands for a raise from any position. Just remember that A-K, even suited, is still a drawing hand, not a made hand. You will usually have to flop something to A-K to make it profitable to continue playing after the flop. Any pair lower than aces can get you into trouble before the flop if you don't play it properly. If someone is willing to put a lot of money in the pot before the flop, even a high pair could be in trouble.

If nobody has entered the pot and I am sitting on the button or right in front it, I will usually raise with any hand that has two cards 10 or higher in it. This means that hands like J-10, Q-10, A-J, A-10, K-J, K-Q, K-10, A-Q and pocket tens become raising hands from a late position. Naturally, the top five starting hands are also raising hands. If someone re-raises me, I will have to decide whether to continue playing or fold. When a player calls a raise with a suited ace with a small kicker such as A-5, for example, he can be up against a hand that also contains an ace with a bigger kicker. When this happens, the player with the A-5 is dominated by the ace-big kicker, and has only three **outs** (three ways to make a better hand)—the three remaining fives. Of course, a draw to a flush or a straight could also develop, but that is not what happens most of the time. The point is that you should not call raises with this type of hand.

WINNING TIP #2
Play Fewer Hands than You Play in Limit Hold'em

To be a successful no-limit hold'em player, you don't need to play a lot of hands, but you do need to win the majority of the hands you decide to play. Many hands that play reasonably well in limit hold'em—hands such as A-Q, K-J suited, pocket tens and suited connectors in multiway pots—do not play nearly as well in no-limit hold'em. The reason that these marginal hands don't hold up very well in no-limit hold'em is because your opponent can make a big enough bet to make it unprofitable for you to continue playing your hand. In limit hold'em, where you and your opponents are restricted to a limited number of fixed bets and raises, you usually do not have to put your entire stack of chips in jeopardy on any one hand. This is not the case in no-limit hold'em, a game in which you can lose your entire stack on one bet.

Because you can lose all your chips on one hand, cards such as the A-Q and K-J that I mentioned above can be extremely troublesome and difficult to play in no-limit hold'em. For example, suppose a player raises in early position and you are on the button with A-Q. You think to yourself, "I have two big cards and position on this raiser. I'll call him and see what develops." The flop comes with A-10-5 **rainbow** (three different suits). Now you say to yourself, "Wow, I have top pair with a pretty good kicker. Yummy!" Your opponent, the one who raised in early position, checks to you. "Well now, I'll just make about a pot-sized bet here," you think. "I probably have the best hand so I might as well make a bet and try to win some more of good ol' Joe's money." You make the bet and good ol' Joe studies you for a moment, staring at you intensely. Then he makes an announcement you don't want to hear: "I'm raising you all in!" Now what do you do?

You're probably drawing to just three outs, the three queens that are left in the deck, to win the pot. If you had been studying your opponent and had determined that he was a tight player, you probably should have folded your hand before the flop against his early-position raise. This is just one example of the problems that can develop in the play of no-limit hold'em if you try to play the same types of hands you are accustomed to playing in limit hold'em. Whereas only a few extra bets could be in jeopardy when you play a mediocre hand in limit hold'em, your entire stack of chips can be ruined when you play marginal cards in no-limit hold'em.

WINNING TIP #3
Learn How Much to Raise

One of the most common mistakes that new players make in no-limit hold'em is betting the wrong amount of chips when they raise. New players usually do one of two things—they either underbet the pot or they overbet it. That is, they bet too few chips or too many chips. Either of these mistakes can get you into trouble.

Underbetting the pot is a very common mistake that beginning hold'em players make, especially when they first start the transition from playing limit hold'em. Oftentimes I see several people enter the pot for the minimum bet, which is always the size of the big blind. Then someone in late position makes a raise exactly double the size of the big blind, which is a very weak play. Raising such a small amount won't drive any of the original callers out of the pot, and could give one of the early limpers an opportunity to make a much bigger raise, forcing everyone out of the pot. Why not simply call and see what develops after the flop? Having late position gives you the advantage on all future betting rounds.

Overbetting the pot is another common mistake. Suppose the blinds are $10/$20 and nobody has entered the pot yet. You look down and find two beautiful aces, the best possible starting hand. You get excited, your heart starts beating faster and you announce, "I raise!" as you shove $500 into the pot. Everyone folds, including the blinds, and you have just won the pot. Winning the pot is good, of course, except for one minor detail—you have only made a $35 profit with the best possible starting hand. What happened? You made the mistake of overbetting the pot and forcing everyone out. If you had bet a little less—around $100—you might have gotten a caller and won a bigger pot. It's true that you could also have gotten outdrawn and lost with your aces, but that's a chance you must take. After all, you can't make an omelet without breaking a few eggs, and you can't be a winner at no-limit hold'em unless you can make the most profit out of your strong starting hands.

So, how much should you raise when you enter the pot in no-limit hold'em? As a general guideline, raise three to four times the size of the big blind. For example, if the big blind is $20, raise to $60 or $80.

WINNING TIP #4
Play Very Few Hands from an Early Position

The earlier your position in relation to the big blind, the worse it is for you. The later your position, the better it is for you. Why? It is very simple. As we explained in limit hold'em, when you are the last player to act, you know what everybody is doing before the action gets to you. This is a big advantage. If you are the first to act, all the other players have an edge on you because you have to act on your hand before they do. This means that many hands that are playable in late position are not playable in early position.

If you enter the pot from early position with the 10♣ 9♣, for example, you don't know whether someone will raise after you enter the pot. This could make that type of hand too expensive to play for profit. Hands with middle-rank connecting cards need lots of callers and, preferably, no preflop raise to make them worthwhile to play. In a nutshell, the earlier you have to act the less information you have, and the later you have to act, the more information you have.

Most players, even professional players, lose money by playing hands in the first two seats after the big blind. Only the best starting hands like big pairs and A-K can be played for a long-term profit from early position. Small pairs and suited connectors just do not play well from an early position.

WINNING TIP #5
Learn the Playing Styles of Your Opponents as Soon as Possible

Poker is a people game played with cards, not a card game played with people. This means that you need to learn how to play your cards against the different types of opponents you are likely to face at the poker table. You will often play your hand one way against a tight conservative player, and a completely different way against a loose aggressive player. For example, say that you have the A-J of clubs and are sitting on the button. Tight Ted, who has not played a hand in over an hour, suddenly raises from an early position. What kind of hand do you think he has? By his previous play, he has showed you that he doesn't play very many hands. Now he has cards he likes enough to raise with from an early position. What should you do?

I know what I would do—I'd fold my hand in a New York minute against this type of player in this situation. I would be afraid that I was up against a big pair or A-K, which would make it very difficult for me to win the pot. Now let's say that you have the same hand and again you are the button. Everybody folds to the player on your immediate right (the cut-off seat) and he raises. In fact Rammin' Robert has raised the last three hands in a row and has played over 50 percent of the hands dealt to him. What do you think of his raise and what should you do? Again, I know what I would do against Robert—I'd reraise him. I probably have not only a better starting hand, I also have position on him. By reraising him I can probably force the blinds to throw their hands away, an added bonus for raising, and get it heads-up between me and the raiser.

The point is that against the tight player, I would fold, but against the loose player, I would raise. In other words I would play the very same hand totally differently depending upon the playing style of my opponent. Learning the playing styles of all your opponents will accelerate your success at the poker table.

WINNING TIP #6
Learn How to Bluff in the Right Situations

The bluff is a major element in playing no-limit hold'em success-fully. However many new players make the classic mistake of bluff-ing too often, probably because they've been watching too much television poker. The World Poker Tour on the Game Show Net-work (GSN) and the World Series of Poker on ESPN bring all the top poker action right into your living room. What you are watch-ing, however, is usually just the final-table action, not the play that allowed the finalists to get there. When the audience sees players raising each other with hands like 4-3, or moving all their chips into the center of the table with nothing but a flush draw, they think that's how to play the game. In other words, the audience is led to believe that players bluff far more often in no-limit hold'em that they actually do.

The truth is that final-table action is quite a bit different from the play in the early stages of the tournament. Players have less rea-son to bluff in the opening rounds of the tournament because the blinds are much smaller and, therefore, they can afford to wait for strong starting hands. But at the final table, it's a different story because the blinds are very high—it simply costs too much to just sit and wait for a powerful hand. Therefore, the players must try to maneuver each other out of the pot just to survive. This means that they sometimes attack each other with much weaker hands. The bottom line is that what might be a correct bluffing situation in the final stages of the tournament could get you broke in the earlier stages.

Timing is everything in executing a successful bluff. That is why getting to know your opponents is so important. Tighter players will often surrender their blinds without much of a fight. These players are easier to bluff. Loose players who frequently defend their blinds and play lots of pots are much harder to bluff. They will gamble with you. Know your man, get your hand, and then bluff!

WINNING TIP #7
Don't Stick With a Hand that Has Come Unglued

One of the most common mistakes that new players make is not folding a great starting hand that has been drawn out on. This usually happens when a player who started with a big pair such as aces or kings has raised before the flop and bet again on the flop. Then a straight card or a flush card comes on fourth street. An opponent makes a big bet at the pot or even check-raises—and yet the preflop raiser continues playing the hand when it obviously is beaten. Here's the message: You must be able to fold a great hand once in a while to preserve your precious stack of chips. It doesn't matter if your opponent started with a much weaker hand than yours—if you're beaten, you must fold.

Another great hand that often goes awry is a pocket pair to which you flopped a set. A set will win around 80 percent of the time, a very high percentage indeed. However if your set gets drawn out on, it can become very expensive unless you have the discipline to fold your hand and avoid getting broke to it. Suppose you start with pocket sevens and the flop comes K-Q-7 with two diamonds. With a flop like that, there could be both flush and straight draws out against you. Now the turn card comes and a four of clubs hits the board. You bet again and still get called. The river card is the jack of diamonds, making both a possible flush and a possible straight. An opponent, known for his tight play, moves a mountain of chips to the center of the pot. What could he have? Judging from the way he played the hand, he almost certainly has a flush, probably the nut flush. If he made a straight, and didn't believe you were playing a flush draw since you bet twice instead of just checking to get a free card, he would probably bet a straight also. Either way you're beaten. Therefore you must fold to preserve your chips.

WINNING TIP #8
Raise More Often than You Call

This tip defines one of the major differences between limit hold'em and no-limit hold'em. No-limit hold'em is a bettor's game not a caller's game. Anytime you make a bet, especially a large bet, you are putting your opponent to a test. Anytime your opponent makes a big bet at you, he is putting you to a test. It is much better to be the tester than the tested. In other words you want to be the one who forces your opponent to guess what you have and make a decision based on speculation rather than the other way around. Most of the time he will guess wrong.

Many times you are faced with the decision to call another player's bet, fold to his bet, or raise. Of these three options, calling is usually the worst. Many times it is a choice between folding or raising—and raising often is the best option. Players frequently raise with less than premium starting hands, but when faced with a re-raise from a solid player like you, they will fold.

Callers usually are losers in no-limit hold'em. Does that mean you always either raise or fold? Of course not. There are times when I suspect that my opponent may be bluffing and therefore I will simply call him down. If I'm wrong and he does have a strong hand, I will save money by not raising. If he is bluffing, he can't call my raise anyway, so a call is the best play. Hey, nobody ever promised that this game was going to be easy!

WINNING TIP #9
Try to Maximize Your Wins and Minimize Your Losses

The concept of making the most money with your strong hands and losing the least money with your weaker hands is a key concept in every form of poker. Hans "Tuna" Lund, an excellent no-limit hold'em champion, thinks of his chips as, "My soldiers that I'm sending into battle. I'm the general of my army and I have to protect my men."

Following his lead, you might look at your stack of chips as being your army, with each individual chip being a member of your battalion. The more chips you have, the greater your strength and ability to attack the enemy. The smaller your chip count, the fewer soldiers you have to fight your battles, making you more vulnerable. Your goal is to preserve and add to your stack of chips, build your army, in both cash games and tournaments. The main difference between the two is that you can always add more chips to your stack between hands in a cash game, but you cannot reach into your pocket for more money during a tournament.

Playing solid poker in no-limit hold'em is the best approach to both cash games and tournaments. A wild, reckless style of play can help you get hold of a lot of chips, but keeping them is another story. Unless you tighten up your play at some point, you will eventually crash and burn.

WINNING TIP #10
Don't Try to Learn How to Play by Watching TV Tournaments
The gap between the skills of "name" players and new players is wider than the Grand Canyon. You've probably watched commercials on TV that advise: "Don't try this at home." The same thing goes for trying to emulate some of the risky moves you see world-class players make during televised no-limit hold'em tournaments.

Of course, let me contradict myself somewhat by saying that you should sometimes give your opponents more respect than they deserve. Unless you have played with them before, assume that they all know what they're doing. If this proves to be false, you can capitalize on your opponents' lack of skill later in the game. Until I see a player making what I consider to be a very bad play, I pretend that they are all great players.

Put a great deal of emphasis on getting to know the various styles of play that your opponents use, paying special attention to the starting hands they play. Some players obviously deserve more respect than others when they enter a pot, and it is your job to be aware of who these players are so that you can adjust your game accordingly.

I also believe that being polite and respectful to your opponents is necessary. I don't like to see people get angry or upset with each other at the table because it often causes unnecessary tension and even forces some of your opponents to quit the game. In this respect, particularly disregard some of the seemingly rehearsed antics you see a few famous poker players performing on television.

Poker is a fun game, and it is even more fun when people are laughing and having a good time. If your opponents are enjoying themselves, they are less likely to become upset when they lose their money, and will continue playing as long as they are having a good time. Respect others as both people and players.

6. NO-LIMIT HOLD'EM PRACTICE HANDS

My Uncle Clarence was fond of using the expression, "Why reinvent the wheel?" He also liked saying, "If it ain't broke, don't fix it." Taking those two axioms to heart, I am once again collaborating with past World Champion of Poker Tom McEvoy to present the following gems of solid advice. Why would I want to change a thing? Thanks, Uncle, for your good advice. Now here's the best advice available on how to play particular types of no-limit hold'em hands.

In this section you will learn how to play certain kinds of no-limit hold'em hands according to your position in the betting sequence. Whether you are sitting in an early, middle or late position is especially important in no-limit hold'em because you risk your entire stack of chips every time you play a hand, whereas in limit hold'em, you risk only one or more bets that are limited in size.

The number of players who have the advantage of getting to act after you have acted becomes all the more important, especially when you are sitting one or two seats to the left of the big blind. Because your position in the betting sequence is so important in no-limit Texas hold'em, we have divided each Practice Hand into three parts: Early Position, Middle Position, and Late Position.

1. TWO ACES

What is the best hand that you can start with in no-limit hold'em? Aces, of course. But there's an old saying in poker that aces win small pots and lose big pots. I disagree with this old adage, because I believe that if you play aces the right way in all situations, you can win with them more often than you lose. Let's start with how to play A-A from a front position.

EARLY POSITION

People have different ideas on how to play pocket aces when you're sitting in an early table position. Some players like to raise while others prefer just calling. Raising will help you force some of your opponents to fold, meaning that you will have fewer people to beat in order to win the pot. But you take the risk of winning less money when fewer players are in the pot. Just calling the size of the big blind (limping) can deceive your opponents into entering the pot because they think that you have a mediocre hand, so the pot probably will be bigger than it would have been if you had raised. But you take the risk of having to play against more opponents, any one of whom could beat your aces if they have a drawing hand or a lower pair and hit the flop just right.

I don't like my odds of winning with my pocket aces when I have several opponents because I know that pocket pairs stand a better chance against only one or two opponents. Therefore I recommend raising three to four times the size of the big blind when you have pocket aces in an early position.

MIDDLE POSITION

If the pot has been opened or raised by a player sitting in the one of the first three seats to the left of the big blind, you can either reraise or just call. It depends on the kind of game you're playing in. Suppose you're in an action game. A player comes in for the minimum bet, you also just call, two or three other players limp in after you, and then a guy who raises almost every pot puts in a raise. In other words, there are four or five limpers before anybody raises the pot. Good! By just calling, you have set up the raiser up so that you can reraise. If you reraise right there, your opponents might figure that you are just trying to steal the pot, or that you have an A-K, but they hardly ever put you on aces because you just called the first time you had a chance to bet.

LATE POSITION

Always raise or reraise with aces from a late position. After everyone has passed to the button, you sometimes will see people limp with pocket aces. That's not a good idea! The chances that a player will raise from either of the two blinds are slim since you have two of the four aces in the deck locked up. If neither of the blinds raise, they're going to get free cards on the flop with any kind of oddball hand. And then you will have no idea of where you are with your aces when the flop comes with 8-4-3, for example, and one of the blinds bets into you. That's why you should raise with aces when you're in late position.

It doesn't matter how many people already are in the pot, raise. If someone has raised in front of you with a lot of players in the pot, reraise. You cannot give free cards very often (especially in a tournament) if you want to win. A lot of times, too, your opponents will discount the strength of your hand when you make a late-position raise and they will play with you because they believe that you're just trying to steal the pot.

Any time that you have pocket aces, you want someone to come after you with a raise. Then your decision is whether to just flat-call and try to nail him after the flop, or move in immediately to try to win the pot right there. If you flat-call, there's always the danger that your opponent will out-flop you. When you're playing aces in no-limit poker, you're always trying to maximize the amount of money that you can win with your hand, so you should choose the strategy that will best serve that purpose.

THE BLINDS

It's great to be dealt pocket aces, but the worst place you can get them is in the small blind or the big blind. Why? Because you're in the weakest table position of all at the start of the hand. After the flop, you will always have to act first. Therefore, when you have pocket aces in one of the blinds, it is more important to raise than it is from any other position to try to get as many other players to fold their hands as possible. Most reasonable players will pay attention when one of the blinds raises, because they know that he must have a very strong hand.

Now suppose everybody checks to the button. He raises and the small blind folds. You're sitting in the big blind with pocket aces. How do you play them in this situation? You might try to trap him by just flat-calling the raise in the hope that something will come on the flop that hits him a little bit but hits you even better. For example, he might have raised with a hand such as A-6 and think that he has the best hand if either an ace or a six hits the flop.

To summarize, pocket aces is such a powerful hand that you raise with them most of the time from any position, no matter what other players do in front of you or behind you. And then you pray that lady luck will deal just the right flop!

2. TWO KINGS

You've been dealt two kings, the second-best starting hand in no-limit Texas hold'em. You're ready to shout for joy—but wait! Pocket kings can be one of the most dangerous hands in poker. Why? Because it is so hard to fold before the flop if an opponent puts in a big raise. And if somebody with an ace in his hand calls when you raise before the flop, you're a goner if an ace comes on the flop.

So, how do you play pocket kings? Usually, if an opponent raises in front of you, reraise with your two kings. Of course, there's always the chance that you will run into two aces, or a **big ace** (an ace with a big card), or even any ace, but that's a chance you'll just have to take in a cash game. But in a tournament, any time the flop is raised and reraised before it gets to you, you're probably better off folding your two kings. Even if you are wrong once in a while, you'll save a lot of money in the long run.

EARLY POSITION

Suppose you're playing in a $50 buy-in no-limit hold'em tournament and you are in the middle stage of the event. You are Player A, the first to act, and you have been dealt pocket kings. How do you play the hand before the flop?

You can raise three or four times the size of the big blind, or you can just call with the two kings from a front position in the hope that someone will raise. The reason that you might just call with the kings is to let somebody raise behind you so that you can re-raise and win the pot right there. If somebody behind you has pocket aces and raises the pot, there's nothing you can do about it. You're caught between a rock and a hard place, so you just call the reraise and wait to see if a handsome cowboy comes out of hiding on the flop. If a player just calls your raise, you still have the second-best hand that you can start with. Just hope that no ace comes on the board.

Say that you limp with the kings, Player B raises, and Player C calls the raise. What should you do? Reraise about the size of the pot. More than likely, you will win the pot right there, unless either Player B or C has aces or queens. If either one of them reraises you, you're in trouble. If Player B has aces, for example, he will move you all-in, but if he doesn't do that, there's a pretty good chance that you have the best hand.

MIDDLE POSITION

Play pocket kings from a middle position similar to how you would play aces. Your main goal is to eliminate other players, especially the ones who are in a later position that you. You want to play your pocket kings head-up against just one opponent.

If there are lots of action players in the game who haven't acted yet, you can just call with the intention of reraising. But if the people who get to act after you are tight players, definitely raise three to four times the size of the big blind if you are the first one in the pot. If a player has raised in front of you, almost always reraise. If you reraise and an opponent moves all in against your reraise, you will have a big decision to make. Does he have pocket aces or could he have a lesser pair? In no-limit hold'em, when an opponent puts all his chips into the pot after two players have already raised in front of him, you can be sure that he has a big hand. How big is the question.

LATE POSITION

Play pocket kings from a late table position almost the same way you would play aces. Never limp into the pot with them. You want any player who has a big ace to fold. You also want anyone who has a smaller pair or a small ace to fold. When I refer to a player with a big ace or one with a small ace, I am referring to the rank of his kicker. An A-Q, for example, is a big ace. An A-4 is a small ace.

Pocket kings is a more vulnerable hand than pocket aces, of course. When you have kings, there are four aces in the deck that could beat you on the flop. And that is why you need to protect your kings as much as you can by raising or reraising before the flop.

3. TWO QUEENS

Two queens is sometimes a very difficult hand to play in no-limit hold'em. It's almost always too good to fold but it's also very vulnerable against A-K, as well as K-K and A-A. Often, your success in a tournament depends on the times when you push with queens and the times when you fold them. If you're not mentally prepared to fold two queens when you need to, you'd better not be playing no-limit hold'em. There are a lot of scenarios where pocket queens is a great hand, but there also are a lot of situations where it isn't.

EARLY POSITION

Do not slowplay queens from an early position because any ace or king that comes on the flop will put you in jeopardy. You want to bring them in for a raise in order to get some money into the pot. But if a player reraises a substantial portion of his chips before the flop, pocket queens is not the type of hand that you want to take a stand with. You should release them in this scenario. Making laydowns when it is correct to do so is just as important as making the right calls and raises.

Suppose you have pocket queens against one opponent and the flop comes J-8-2. You make a bet and he calls. You can beat hands such as A-J, Q-J, and 10-9. Ask yourself, "What cards could my opponent have?" He may have pocket eights or a straight draw. Or he may have slowplayed (just called before the flop) with aces or kings. Suppose a 4 comes on the turn. Should you check or bet? Queens is not a hand that you can afford to give a free card with. Go ahead and bet again. If you check, you face the possibility that an ace or king will come on the river and you will lose a hand that you should have won. Generally speaking, never give a free card when you have the best hand, especially in tournaments.

MIDDLE POSITION

Pocket queens is not a big enough hand to just call with. Your main goal is to eliminate players and try to win the hand either before the flop or on the flop. Therefore you need to make a big enough raise so that it will be unprofitable for the opposition to call and get a chance to draw out against you.

If one or two people have already limped into the pot, make your raise more than three or four times the size of the big blind. For example, suppose the blinds are $25/$50 and two people in front of you have just called for $50. It's your turn to act, so make it around $300 to go. If someone has raised in front you—for example, they have made it $200 to go—make it about $600 to go.

If you get called and neither an ace nor a king comes on the flop, you can make a pot-sized bet and try to win the hand right there. If you get called, you will need to decide what type of hand your opponent has and act accordingly on the next round of betting. As you can see, pocket queens can be a tough hand to play at times.

LATE POSITION

If you hold queens in late position or on the button and a few players have limped in front of you, your queens increase in value. The chances are that no players behind you (the blinds) have bigger pairs than yours. In this situation, always raise with pocket queens. Then if the flop comes with small cards, you can try to win the pot right there.

Your biggest decision when you have pocket queens is not how to play them when you have the best hand, but whether you can fold them when you have the worst hand.

Pocket queens is the third-best starting hand in hold'em, but always remember that as the rank of your pair gets smaller, there are more higher pairs and overcards that can beat your hand.

4. JACKS AND TENS

Jacks and tens are two of the most difficult hands to play in no-limit hold'em. Although you'd rather have pocket jacks than tens, one advantage of tens is that a 10 can make a straight, and it is less likely that someone else can make a straight because you have two of them in your hand. Just remember that if you don't flop a set when you have pocket tens, there are four bigger cards that can beat you. So if an overcard hits the flop, you can't play your hand with any confidence. Precisely with tens, you are a "favorite" to have one or more overcards on the flop, whereas with jacks, it's about even money. My thanks to T.J. Cloutier for the following advice on playing jacks and tens, adapted from his and McEvoy's book, *Championship Hold'em Tournament Hands*.

If you are the first one in the pot, you can bring it in for a raise. If you are reraised, do not hesitate to throw your tens away. Now suppose there is a limper in early position and you are in second position. Should you raise with pocket tens? I am very leery of raising in this spot because if I get raised by a player sitting behind me, I probably don't have the best hand. However, if there is a limper in early position and you're sitting in one of the last two seats, you definitely can raise with pocket tens. If the limper comes back over the top, you can fold.

Suppose that you have pocket jacks or tens one spot in front of the button (the cutoff seat). You raise and the big blind calls.

The board comes:

The big blind checks to you and you bet. Then the big blind re-raised.

What do you do?

You can't possibly like your hand when someone raises you. Your opponent either thinks you're on a steal, or he has a big hand and is trying to suck you in. If you have only a relatively small amount of chips left in a tournament, you might call, but if you have a lot of chips, you probably should pass. There are situations when your opponent might raise with a pair of nines or eights or an A-7, for example. If you know how he plays, you should be able to decide whether to continue with the hand or simply fold. In other words, be very cautious when you flop an overpair to the board. You can bet, of course, but if someone raises, you might be in a dangerous situation.

EARLY TO MIDDLE POSITION

From early to middle position, you can raise with pocket jacks or tens, especially if you're the first one in the pot. Just decide in advance that you aren't going to call a raise. If someone raises behind you, it's usually time to bail out. You also can limp with pocket jacks or tens from early to middle position. If anyone raises before the flop, usually pass. For example, in the early stages of a big buy-in tournament when lots of chips are in play, just calling a minimum bet certainly is a viable strategy. On the flop, you want to hit a set—and if you don't, you can get away from them without losing much money because you only limped before the flop.

LATE POSITION

Suppose you are in late position, five or six players have passed, and then one player enters the pot for the minimum bet. In this scenario, you should bring it in for a raise with pocket jacks or tens.

How you play jacks or tens in a tournament is always a question of using the best tournament strategy. There are times in tournaments when you might play tens like you would play deuces—especially in the early stages of a big buy-in tournament when lots of chips are in play and the blinds are small. Other times, in the later stages of the tournament, you might have to go all in with your tens because of your chip position. If you aren't willing to modify your style of play according to the situation, you can get broke to jacks or tens very easily.

5. MIDDLE AND SMALL PAIRS

MIDDLE PAIRS

The bigger the pocket pair the better off you are, and the smaller the pair the more vulnerable you are. However, there isn't a lot of difference in how you play any of the middle pairs—nines, eights, and sevens—and you play them similar to the way that you play tens. You can raise with them from late position if you are the first one in the pot, but be prepared to pitch them if you get played with. If you get called, play them very cautiously after the flop. You cannot stand much pressure from other players when you have a middle pair, and you don't want to play too aggressively either.

In tournaments, your chip position often dictates how you play middle pairs. There are times when you are forced to play them— for example when you are very low on chips and believe that you probably won't get a better hand to play. This is about the only time when you take a stand with middle pairs (go all in).

SMALL PAIRS

Suppose you have made it to the final table in a no-limit hold'em tournament. The table is six-handed and you look down at pocket sixes on the button. The action is passed to you. What do you do?

In this situation, it might be okay to make a small raise with your low pair. For example, say that the antes are $200 and the blinds are $400/$800 at a six-handed table. There is $2,400 in the pot. You have $15,000 in front of you. If you want to raise, why not bring it in for $3,000? If you get reraised, you can fold the hand before the flop. And if you get out-flopped, you can fold the hand right there. But what are you going to do if you move in your whole stack and get called? This is why you should play small pairs even more cautiously than you play medium pairs.

If you have two sixes, for example, and your opponent has an 8-7, the 8-7 is only a slight underdog to your pair of sixes. In fact, any two overcards are only a small underdog to a pair. And if the overcards are suited, they are a slightly smaller dog to the pair. This is why you should not play very aggressively with a low pocket pair.

6. ACE-KING

To win a no-limit hold'em tournament, you have to win with A-K and you have to beat A-K. Although it may not be the final hand, A-K often will be the deciding hand, the one with which you win or lose the most chips. Big Slick is the biggest "decision" hand in tournament play.

A-K is a drawing hand, not a made hand. You will flop a pair to A-K about 30 percent of the time. If you go to the river with it, you will make a pair about 50 percent of the time. I believe that A-K is the most frequently misplayed hand in no-limit hold'em. Players call with it in situations where a raise would be the better play. They move in with A-K when they probably should fold. And they often misplay A-K after the flop. Big Slick can be a very profitable hand, but it also can send you to the rail.

EARLY POSITION

When I am sitting in an early position, I like to make a standard raise of three to four times the size of the big blind if I am the first player to enter the pot. If I'm playing in the early stage of a tournament and an opponent makes a big reraise before the flop, I usually will fold. If only one player has entered the pot before it is my turn to act, I will raise if I suspect that my opponent is weak. But if I suspect that he has a big hand and is just trying to trap me, I will just flat-call his bet. Knowing how your opponents play will help you in making decisions like this.

MIDDLE POSITION

When you are sitting in a middle position at the table, raise the standard amount if you are the first player in the pot—don't ever just flat-call. A-K is not a hand that you should slowplay in this situation because it is a drawing hand, not a made hand. But if two or more people have limped into the pot for the minimum bet, be inclined to just call, especially if you're playing in the early stage of a tournament. What if only one person has limped into the pot? You can either raise or just flat-call depending on what kind of hand strength you think your opponent has.

If the pot has been raised before it gets to me, I usually will just call and see the flop. If the flop gives my A-K no help whatsoever, I will fold if someone bets.

LATE POSITION

The betting action that has happened before it is my turn to act is the determining factor in how I play A-K when I am sitting in a late position at the table. If one player has raised from an early position and two players have called the raise, I usually will also call. I want to see what develops on the flop. But if someone has moved in all his chips before it's my turn to act, I will fold.

What if no one has entered the pot and I am on or next to the button? In that case, I will raise. And if only one or two of my opponents have entered the pot for the minimum bet, I will raise if I think they are weak players. It's a lot easier to decide what to do with Big Slick when you're in late position, isn't it? Ditto for a lot of other hands.

THE BLINDS

Seldom raise from either of the blinds if two or more limpers already are in the pot. You don't have good position after the flop—in fact, you have the worst position at the table—and if you get reraised, you could be in a ton of trouble. One of the advantages of not raising with A-K is that you often will get action from lesser hands if you flop top pair. Players are accustomed to seeing the opposition raise with A-K, so they probably won't give you credit for having such a strong hand since you didn't raise with it before the flop.

Should you ever raise with A-K from one of the blinds? Yes, when you are the small blind and nobody has entered pot, meaning that you will be playing the hand head-up against the big blind. In that case, raise the standard amount. Another time when you might raise is when you are the big blind and the small blind has called for half a bet. If you think he has a weak hand, make a standard raise.

7. ACE-QUEEN AND ACE-JACK

ACE-QUEEN

A-Q is a trouble hand that you should play cautiously. You don't
want to put a lot of money in the pot with A-Q (suited or unsuited)
from an early position. Treat being suited as a bonus, something
that should not change how you play the hand. Although I prefer
suited cards when I play an A-Q, A-J or A-10, I value their ranks
more than their suitedness.

You cannot stand a reraise before the flop with A-Q in the opening rounds of a tournament. If you are sitting in middle to late
position and there are other limpers in the pot, you can call with
A-Q in order to see the flop cheaply. If nobody has entered the
pot, raise a modest amount of about three times the size of the big
blind. If anyone reraises, fold. If you flop top pair, usually make
a pot-sized bet on the flop. Later in the tournament, particularly
when you're playing at a shorthanded table, A-Q goes up in value.
When you're either short stacked or are up against a short stack,
you might even have to go all in with the hand.

ACE-JACK

A-J and A-10 are even more troublesome to play than A-Q. You
can't afford to call any raises with these hands before the flop. A-J
is a little bit stronger than A-10 because of its higher kicker. A-10
gains some value from the 10. Although it is a weak kicker, the
10 can make a straight. Being suited is strictly a bonus. Generally
speaking, these are calling hands from middle to late position when
others have entered the pot for the minimum bet. You sometimes
can raise with them from late position when no one has entered,
but discard them if anyone reraises.

8. ACE-WHEEL CARD

An ace with a small card, suited or unsuited, is not a hand that you should play from an early position. It is of little value to you there. Why? Because if an ace comes on the flop and you bet—and an opponent calls or raises—you have a bad kicker and are in danger of losing to an ace with a high kicker. Obviously the best flop for ace-small suited is three to your suit or three wheel cards. But the odds are so great against getting that kind of flop that if you play ace-small every time you are dealt it, you will be a big loser.

Now suppose you are in middle to late position and a couple of limpers are in the pot. Since it is developing into a multiway pot, you might just call and see the flop cheaply. If you get a good flop to it in multiway action, you have the chance to win a nice pot. You don't want to call a raise with A-4 and you don't want to play it heads up. Therefore when you call for the minimum bet, be prepared to throw your hand away if someone raises.

Suppose you're on the button and no one has entered the pot. Should you raise with ace-small? No. Suppose the small blind calls the raise. What could he have? He probably has an ace in his hand or a pocket pair. And almost any kicker that he has with his ace will be higher than your wheel card. Even if his kicker also is a wheel card, you still are not a favorite to the hand most of the time if an ace falls on the flop.

When you are in the small blind against the big blind only, you have three options: raise, fold or call. If you just call, you might get yourself into trouble. If you fold, you stay out of trouble. If you raise, you might win the pot right there. It depends on how you feel about it. For example, if you have observed that your opponent typically defends his blind, usually just complete the bet against this type of opponent. If he is someone who raises all the time, he might raise just because you limped. What you decide to do depends on the type of player your opponent is.

What about playing hands like A-6, A-7, or A-8? None of these ace-middle-card hands can make a straight. Your best result is the nut flush if the hand is suited, or two pair if you hit your kicker. You're just throwing your money away if you play them.

9. KING-QUEEN

In no-limit hold'em, K-Q is a trap hand. Unless you flop something like J-10-9, A-J-10, two kings and a queen, or even two pair, you will be in bad shape with this hand. K-Q is a hand that you don't want to play in a nine-handed ring game, in particular, from an early or a middle position. I give a little more value to J-10 because you can make more straights with the hand than you can make with either K-Q or Q-J.

LATE POSITION

Suppose you're playing in a $100 tournament and are dealt K-Q. The action is passed to you on the button. How do you play the hand? You might raise to try to knock out the two blinds, but that is the only circumstance in which you should consider raising with it. Although K-Q suited is better than K-Q offsuit, being suited doesn't increase its value very much. It is still the type of hand that can get you into big trouble.

Now suppose you are on the button with K-Q and a player raises in front of you. What do you do? You can get into trouble if you call the raise. Fold.

K-Q IN THE BLINDS

Suppose you are in the little blind with a K-Q. Everybody else has passed. Now what do you do? In this case, you can raise the big blind, even though you are out of position and will have to act first after the flop. Some players will call a small raise from the big blind with hands that aren't very good because they already have money in the pot, but the chances are good that you'll win the pot right there with your preflop raise.

10. MIDDLE SUITED CONNECTORS

Middle connectors are hands that you play in cash games to try to win a big pot in multiway action. But in tournaments, you face a big problem with these types of hands—you can't put more money on the table when you lose all your chips like you can in cash games. When you lose your stack, you're out of action. And that is why you seldom play middle connectors in tournaments.

EARLY POSITION

You simply do not play hands such as 9-8, 8-7 or 7-6, suited or offsuit, from an early position in no-limit hold'em because you cannot call a raise with them. Furthermore, you will be in a bad betting position from the flop onward. Always remember that the chips you do not lose on mediocre hands in bad position will be available to you later to possibly double or triple up with on your good hands.

LATE POSITION

When two or more players have entered the pot for the minimum bet, you can occasionally play middle connectors from the cutoff seat or the button. But suppose everyone passes to you on the button and you have the 9♥ 8♥. What do you do? Fold. Remember that if nobody in front of you has a hand, somebody behind you might have one. I call it the **bunching factor**, meaning that if no one has big cards in front of you, it is somewhat more likely that big cards are "bunched" behind you.

The only other time that it might be okay to play hands such as 9♥ 8♥ in no-limit hold'em is when you hold them in the big blind in an unraised pot. You also can call for one-half a bet from the small blind. However if the big blind raises, throw the hand away. Remember that a lot of people play ace-anything—A-10, A-9, A-8—for the minimum bet so that if you hit a 9 or 8 on the flop, the chances are good that someone will have a better kicker. Just because any two cards can win in hold'em doesn't mean that you should play them.

7. WINNING AT LOW-LIMIT OMAHA HIGH-LOW

Omaha high-low was invented by a sadist and is played by masochists. "It ain't my cup of tea," Uncle Clarence once told me. "You've gotta' sit there and wait for the absolute nuts, wade through all them slow betting rounds, get drawn out on by trash hands and then split the pot. I'd rather play Go Fish with my grandson!"

Sometimes I think he's right—but I love this intriguing brand of hold'em poker. If you're a novice at Omaha high-low, or if you've been playing the low-limit games for a while without scoring many wins, the tips in this book will help you to accelerate your climb to the top of the dive-survive-strive-thrive pyramid.

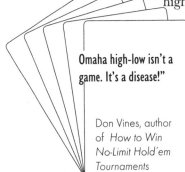

Omaha high-low isn't a game. It's a disease!"

Don Vines, author of *How to Win No-Limit Hold'em Tournaments*

THE BASICS OF PLAY

Since Omaha high-low is a form of hold'em, it is played according to the same basic procedures as limit hold'em, no-limit hold'em, and even pot-limit hold'em. Because low-limit Omaha high-low is played with prescribed betting limits, it is more similar to limit hold'em than no-limit hold'em. The main difference between Omaha games and limit hold'em games is the number of cards you are dealt. Instead of receiving two hole cards like you do in hold'em, you receive four hole cards in Omaha.

Another important difference is that in hold'em, you may use zero, one or two cards to make your best hand. In Omaha high-low, you must use exactly two of your four hole cards and exactly three of the board cards to make your best hand. Also, hold'em is a high game. The only time the pot is divided between two or more players is when all active players have hands of equal value. In Omaha high-low, the pot is usually split between the best high hand and the best low hand. The only time the best high hand wins the entire pot is when no low hand is possible; that is, three or more of the board cards are higher than 8.

With these major differences in mind, let's take a short review tour of the basic play of Omaha high-low.

The two players sitting to the left of the button must post blind bets before the deal. The small blind bet must be equal to one-half the small bet, and the big blind bet must be equal to the small bet. For example, in a $4/$8 game, the small blind posts $2 and the big blind posts $4. These mandatory bets are designed to stimulate action by ensuring that players will have some money in the pot to compete for before the flop. Even in the unlikely event that everybody else folds, you figure to have at least the big blind to compete against before the flop. In my experience playing $2/$4, $4/$8 and $5/$10 Omaha high-low, you will have a lot more competition than just the big blind. The number of players who enter pots in low-limit games ranges from four to seven in 9- or 10-handed games. Sometimes everyone joins the fun before the flop, in which case it's called a **family pot**.

As soon as the dealer has raked all the bets to the center of the table, he deals each player four cards face down. These pocket cards are for you alone to see and play. They are the cards that you will be using to make your best possible hand when you combine them with the board cards. Naturally, no two hands can be exactly alike in both suit and rank, but two hands may be identical in rank alone. For example, you could be dealt the A♣ K♣ 2♦ 3♦ while someone else could be dealt the A♠ K♥ 2♣ 3♥.

Play begins with the first player sitting to the immediate left of the big blind and moves clockwise around the table. You have four options when it is your turn to act. You can fold by turning your cards face down and sliding them to the dealer. You can call by placing an amount of money equal to the big blind in front of your hand. You can raise by placing exactly double the amount of the big blind in front of your hand. Or you can reraise by doubling the bet if someone has raised before the action gets to you.

As soon as everyone has acted, the dealer collects all the chips into the pot and deals three cards face up in the center of the table. As in hold'em, this is called the flop. The first person to act is the first active player sitting to the left of the dealer. If both blinds called before the flop, the small blind must act first after flop. The betting then proceeds around the table in the same manner as it did before the flop, with one exception. Each player has the chance to check by announcing, "Check," or by gently rapping the table with his knuckles, denoting that he wants to keep his cards without posting a bet. Sometimes nobody bets on the flop, they all check. In that case everybody gets to see the next card for free. But that seldom happens in Omaha high-low. A sequence that often occurs is that the first person checks, the second player bets, a couple of other players call, another player raises, and then the first person either decides to call the raise, reraise or fold.

Again the dealer drags all the bets into the pot and then turns over the fourth board card (the turn card). The betting proceeds as it did on the flop, with active players checking, folding, calling, raising or reraising. When the action on the turn is complete, the dealer again adds the bets to the pot and then turns over the fifth card in the center of the table. This is it, folks —this is the river!

The river is the ultimate judge of success or failure in Omaha high-low. If you make your hand on the river, you're singing. But if you miss your draw on the river, you're sighing, you're crying, you're losing all those bets! The betting sequence is the same as it was on the turn, except that when the betting is complete, every active player turns over his entire hand so that the dealer can call the winning hand(s). The dealer will declare which is the best low hand, which is the best high hand, or which hand has the best of both worlds and wins the whole enchilada, called **scooping**.

THE IMPORTANCE OF THE TWO-PLUS-THREE RULE

The sequence of play for Omaha high-low is simple, just as it is in all forms of hold'em. But many players who are accustomed to playing limit Texas hold'em, in which they can use either one or two of their hole cards to make their best possible hand, have trouble playing Omaha high-low for the first time. Why? Because they often forget that you must use two cards from your hand and three cards from the board to make your hand. Exactly two plus three, no variations allowed, is the Omaha rule. The good news is that you can use any two of your cards to make your best low hand and any two cards to make your best high hand, whether they are the same two or a different two, even if they overlap. And aces can count for either high or low, or both!

Of course, in order for a low hand to be possible, three of the board cards must be an 8 or lower. And you must have two low cards that do not duplicate any of the three board cards to make a low hand. A **wheel** (A-2-3-4-5) is the best possible low hand and, sometimes, it even wins the other half of the pot as the best high hand (a 5-high straight). When calculating your low hand, neither straights nor flushes count against you. If no one meets the minimum qualifications for a low hand, the player who has the best high hand wins the entire pot. You must turn over all four cards to be awarded your share of the pot.

Now let's study ten tips that I believe will help you thrive at my favorite game, Omaha high-low.

TEN WINNING TIPS

WINNING TIP #1
Play Hands in which All Four Cards Work Together

The expert Omaha high-low player looks for a hand in which all four cards work together as a team, similar to the teamwork of a baseball club. If the shortstop misses the ball, the center fielder is there to back him up. But subtract one of the nine players and the team cannot compete at its highest level.

Similarly, when you enter the contest with K-Q-J-3, your team of cards is missing an important fourth connector and is handicapped before it ever begins the game. In my experience at the green felt, it seems that the high straight I am drawing to always misses by the *one* card I am missing when my hand is a three-legged-straight starter.

T.J. Cloutier, who has won World Series of Poker championships in all three forms of Omaha, put it this way in his book, *Championship Omaha*: "Omaha high-low is a hand-value driven game. You should not be entering pots unless all four of your cards work together in some way. You usually don't want to play a hand with three good cards and a **dangler** (a hole card not connected to the other three hole cards) in it because that dangler can put you in a world of misery."

Ideally, these four cards also contain both a high draw and a low draw. For example, the mighty A♠ K♥ 2♠ 3♥ arms a combatant with multiple layers of armor: two high flush draws, one of which is the nuts; one high straight draw, including a nut straight; the wheel draw, which can capture the entire pot; and even top two pair.

The value of Omaha high-low hands is also influenced by table position, because (as in all button games) players who act last have the advantage over players who must act first. Prosperous poker players do not come into the pot up front with weak hands in either Texas hold'em or Omaha high-low, because front position weaklings usually cannot tolerate bullies who mistreat them by raising, reraising, or capping the pot.

Linda Johnson, who gained TV fame as the World Poker Tour floor spokesperson, is a hugely successful Omaha high-low player at the highest limits. In the lessons she gives at sea during Card Player Cruises, she advises beginners to "play hands that will 'play themselves' after the flop, because it is difficult for a novice to out-play a more experienced opponent."

To find a hand that "plays itself," be on the lookout for low hands that have an ace with a deuce and at least one other **wheel card** (ace, 2, 3, 4 or 5), preferably suited. You'll want three low cards in your hand because you so often need that extra card—an out—to make the best possible low hand. High hands should contain four cards in sequence with as few gaps as possible, or a high pair with two related cards (preferably suited).

Low hands are especially powerful in Omaha high-low, and you can play the premium A-2-3-6 or A-3-4-J types of hands from any position and against any raises. But be more cautious with the high hands you play—they are better played in late positions because they are less powerful than premium low hands. Many experienced players will not play any hand that does not contain an A-2 suited with a backup wheel card— or so they tell me. However, even they have been known to stray upon occasion!

You may feel as though you're constrained by a straight jacket because you'll have to wait out myriad deals before catching these primo cards. Use your hiatus from action to watch the other players, noting the types of hands that are winning the pots. You'll soon learn the starting-hand strength necessary to beat the game.

For the best possible advice on the strength of various Omaha high-low starting hands, I highly recommend that you purchase a copy of Bill Boston's book, *Omaha High-Low: Winning Strategies for all 5,278 Omaha High-Low Hands*. Boston spent years running computer simulations for every possible four-card combination. Then he organized the results into charts that are easy to decipher, added his winning advice, and came up with a bestseller.

WINNING TIP 2
Learn to Read the Board
If I were the gambling sort, I might wager that most beginning Omaha high-low players have lost lots of dough by making just one simple mistake: misreading the board cards as they relate to their hole cards. Even the best players occasionally commit this error. One of the most common times that beginners misread the board is when a board card comes along that duplicates (**counterfeits**) one or more of their hole cards.

Take a look at this example and you'll see how it might happen.

THE FLOP

YOUR HAND   **JOE'S HAND**

THELMA'S HAND

Who has the best hand on the flop?

You have two pair (A-A-5-5-K), but Joe has made three kings (K-K-K-A-5).

Who has the best draw on the flop?

Thelma has the nut low (A-2-3-5) with a draw to the wheel if a 4 comes on board.

THE FLOP   **THE TURN CARD**

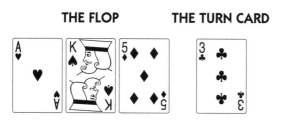

Who has the best hand on the turn?

Joe has the best high hand (K-K-K-A-5).

Thelma has the best low hand (A-2-3-5-6) with a draw to the wheel, plus a draw to a 6-high straight if a 4 comes on the river.

You have two pair with an inside draw to the wheel if a 4 comes on the river, and the best full house if another ace comes.

THE FLOP   THE TURN CARD   THE RIVER

Who has the best hand on the river?

Joe has the best high hand with trip kings: K-K-K-A-7. Thelma has the best low hand (A-2-3-5-6) even though two of her low cards (3 and 5) got counterfeited. Her best high hand was 5-5-3-3-A. You missed your draw for low and missed making a full house, and end up with the same two pair you started with on the flop: A-A-5-5-K.

The Winning Split

Joe wins one-half the pot for high. Thelma wins the other half for low. You win zilch. Better luck next time!

WINNING TIP #3
Fit or Fold

Why do so many amateurs lose so much money at this game? Because they chase pots with beautiful hands that don't match the flop. Beauty does not lie in the hands of the holder, it lies in fitting the flop.

When you enter a pot, ask yourself, "What is the perfect flop for my hand?" Name it to yourself. For example, if you're holding A-2-4-K, you're looking to flop something like A-3-5. Or if you have 2-3-4-5, you might say to yourself, "I need a flop with two low cards and a working ace." You don't want a flop that comes something like A-K-10 because the ace isn't "working" for you. Why? Because it is accompanied by two high cards rather than two low cards. You'd highly prefer seeing a flop something like A-5-6, which would give you the uncounterfeitable nut low, plus a draw to the wheel and a higher straight. Uncounterfeitable nut lows are things of beauty because no matter what other low cards comes on board, you will still have the nut low.

> It's not the hands you play, it's the hands you fold that determine whether or not you'll have a positive bottom line."
>
> Doyle Brunson, 2-time winner of the World Championship of Poker

When the board cards are flopped, ask, "What is the perfect hand for this flop?" If you don't have it, and you don't have a draw to it, fold. You'll save yourself loads of fool's gold if you heed this advice and avoid drawing to long-shots.

Some low-limit and novice players will often chase a flop such as K-Q-3 with hands such as A-2-4-8. If another low card comes on the turn, they're ready to call a raise hoping for a low river card. Look for other outs, such as the A-2 suited to two flush cards on the board, or A-2-4-10, which offers an extra inside straight draw for the above board. Without those extra outs—draws to a back-up hand—fold when your hand does not fit the flop.

WINNING TIP #4
Draw Only to the Nuts

Why do so many players lose so many pots with the second-nut low or the second-best full house, the third-highest flush, or the lowest possible straight? Because they draw to them. Why do they draw to less than the nuts? Because they hope no one else holds the nut hand. They're the players I call optimistic losers. Believe me when I say that in Omaha high-low, the cup is not always half full!

"Hope" is a nasty four-letter word in Omaha high-low. Many players who have written me after reading my book, *Omaha High-Low: How To Win At The Lower Limits*, have said that one of the most useful axioms in the book is: "If it's possible, it's probable." Many "Omaholics" fall into the trap of thinking that a king-high flush will win the pot—but I am living testimony that it usually will not, unless the ace is showing on the board. (I paid my dues on this one early in my Omaha high-low career.)

Low-limit Omaha high-low is a game of the nuts. If you don't have the best possible hand or a draw to it, you're in jeopardy. This is especially true for low hands. Even the nut low can get duplicated in two or even (disaster!) three spots at the table. Leave it to the losers to either draw to, or call bets with, the second-nut low when they have no other winning outs.

If it's possible for someone to have a higher high or a lower low than you do, it is probable that they do. Save this axiom in the hard drive of your computer brain. The possible/probable axiom is one of the reasons why the next winning tip is so important.

WINNING TIP #5
Have a Draw to a Back-Up Hand

Many players enter pots in Omaha high-low with an A-2 "bare," that is, without other viable options. For example, amateurs might play A-2-9-J or A-2-9-9, even in pots that are raised. They've heard so much about A-2 being the best possible low hand, they've forgotten how easily it can be counterfeited. Suppose you have A-2-9-10 in the hole and the board comes A-3-K. Now what do you have? Top pair, with a weak kicker and no back-up draws.

Now let's look at another type of hand. You're sitting close to the button and decide that, with four players already in the pot, you'll take a chance and play the middle-connectors you have in the hole. So you call the bet with 9-9-8-7. The flop comes 7-6-5. "Wow! I'm glad I played this hand," you think as you raise the pot with your 9-high straight. The turn card is an 8. You no longer have the nut straight and you don't have a draw to a higher hand. Now what do you do?

Omaha high-low statistician Bill Boston warns strongly against playing hands with a 9 in them. And that's one reason I put a 9 in each of these examples, to give you a "bonus" tip. As Boston puts it, "The worst three cards (in Omaha high-low)—I call them the "three bandits"—are 9, 8, and 7, which are in more losing hands than any other cards." In fact, the 9-8-7-6 hand ranks 4,691 out of the 5,278 possible starting hands in Omaha high-low.

When your starting cards turn into hurting cards, don't take a loss with them. Toss them if you don't have a second draw to a better hand.

WINNING TIP #6
Play Premium High Hands in Late Position or Unraised Pots Only

Experienced Omaha high-low players look for the best *low* hand, one that can win the whole enchilada with a wheel, whereas hold'em players new to Omaha high-low are accustomed to seeking the best *high* hand, not realizing that high hands lose value in this game.

In his excellent book on Omaha high-low for advanced players, *High-Low Split Poker*, Ray Zee states, "High hands do well in situations where one or no low cards come on the flop. When two or three low cards come, these hands tend to do very poorly."

Be cautious if you flop top set, such as trip queens against a flop like Q-3-4, in which the two low cards are in direct sequence. The low-hand players with a straight or wheel draw will usually play this flop aggressively, making you pay dearly to see if the board pairs. If it does, you'll have the nut full house, of course, but you will also split the pot if another low card falls.

WINNING TIP #7
Still Play Solid Poker in Jackpot Games

In jackpot games, you may be tempted to play more hands containing high pairs in hope of cracking that elusive prize fund with quad jacks or better beaten. If you decide to enter the pot with a high pair, be sure that it also has two connecting cards, preferably suited.

In my experience, most Omaha high-low jackpots have been won by a straight flush getting beaten by a higher straight flush. For this reason, if the jackpot is very big ($30,000 or higher) and I am sitting in a late position, I may play hands with connecting suited cards that I ordinarily would not play (5-5-4-3, for example). However I don't play hands with high pairs and no connectors (such as K-K-8-3), and I don't play either of these types of hands in a raised pot.

Resist temptation. Play solid poker, coming in with premium hands that will win or save you more money in the long run than a jackpot that you hope to win.

WINNING TIP #8
Middle Cards and Low Pairs Are Losers

I can't think of a poker game in which middle cards are winners, can you? In Texas hold'em, they often make the idiot end of a straight and lose to the high end. In seven-card stud, two middle pairs always lose to a high pair-low pair combination. In Omaha high-low, hands such as 8-7-6-5 or 6-6-5-3 are spelled *d-o-g*. You're barking up the wrong tree with them. Wait for something better.

WINNING TIP #9
Omaha High-low is a River Game

You want a flop that gives you either the best possible hand or a draw to that hand. In no other poker game do I hear more people complain, "They drew out on me at the river," than I do in Omaha high-low. Maybe that's one reason why I sometimes think that Omaha high-low is a game enjoyed primarily by masochists.

Although many low-limit players try, it is nearly impossible to raise an opponent out of a pot if he believes that he can win it with a favorable river card. The primary purpose of a raise, therefore, is to build the pot to increase your win. Players with the patience to wait for a premium starting hand can often outrun master strategists who use raising and bluffing ploys to try to force out strong drawing hands.

WINNING TIP #10
Don't Whine When Beauty Meets the Beast

This point is important even when the most beautiful hand you've held in the past two hours gets devoured by the beast at the river. The following hand example from Boston's book on Omaha high-low illustrates this point.

You're in a hand with one other player and the big blind. You have an A-2-4-K with the ace suited to the deuce. Your opponent in middle position is holding an A-3-7-7 with the ace suited to a 7. The big blind is the third player in the pot. He has a 10-9-8-2 with three cards of the same suit (a perfectly horrible hand) which he played because he got to see the flop for free.

The flop came 6-7-8. "Your hand looked great," Boston wrote, "double-suited with an ace-deuce draw. You made a nut low and a king-high spade-flush drawing hand." As it turned out on the river, however, your beauties had a fatal run-in with the beast. Here's what happened.

A jack joined the board on the turn and a deuce washed up on the river. The final board looked like this: 6-7-8-J-2. Your best hand? A-2-4-6-7. The middle player's A-2-3-6-7 nudged you out to win the low half of the pot. And what about the big blind? He won high, of course, with rags that turned into riches when they found a home on the board to make the nut straight.

When beauty meets the beast just when you thought it was safe (remember *Jaws*?), you can whimper, you can whine, and then you can go on tilt. Or you can simply wince, wash it out of your mind, and win the next beauty you look down at in the new hand that you'll be dealt in just a matter of minutes. Be a winner, not a whiner!

ANOTHER WORD FROM P.C.

"But Shane, you haven't talked about strategic ploys, when to check an A-2, position plays, slowplaying, and other winning stratagems," my ubiquitous poker conscience is protesting.

"Get off my back, P.C.," I answer. "We both know that if you play premium hands and draw only to the nuts, you usually can win money at this game, no matter what limits you play."

With that, P.C. bids me a reluctant adios until the next chapter.

8. OMAHA HIGH-LOW PRACTICE HANDS

I've selected a few Omaha high-low practice hands that illustrate classic situations you may encounter during your initial journey through the treacherous mine fields of split pots, second-best highs, counterfeited lows, back-up draws and "nutsmanship."

When you're ready to venture deeper into the finer points of Omaha high-low, I recommend three books that will help you immensely. First, *Omaha High-Low: How to Win at the Lower Limits*, my book for novice players. Then move right along to Bill Boston's *Omaha High-Low: Winning Strategies for all 5,278 Omaha High-Low Hands*, followed by Ray Zee's book for advanced players, *High-Low Split Poker*.

Now let's move right along to the job at hand and explore how you might play your cards in the following strategic situations. As Linda Johnson, founder of *Card Player* magazine, is famous for saying at the close of each of her poker columns: "Now, let's play poker!"

1. PLAYING STRAIGHTS AND FLUSHES

When the flop has two or three unsuited cards that give you eight to 16 outs to make the nut straight, you are in good shape. But beware! It is not unusual for two running flush cards to appear on the board on **fourth street** and **fifth street** (the turn and river, respectively), and void the value of your straight. For this reason, some expert players do not play straights (especially middle-card straights) fast. That is, they don't raise or reraise with made middle straights unless they also have a backup flush draw.

Heads up, they might fire away, but smart opponents will not drive a medium nut straight until the river. In fact, they will fold it on the flop if they believe that it has a negative expectation of holding up on the river. Take a look at this hand and the flop, which Expert Eddie played from the button in an unraised pot.

EXPERT EDDIE'S HAND   **THE FLOP**

Even with his made straight, an expert player will not bet this hand fast. He will play it cautiously. Why? Because there are so few "safe" cards remaining. A **safe card** is one that will help your hand, not hurt it. In this example, another heart makes a flush possible for someone else, and a 9 makes a jack-high straight possible. Eddie would need two running cards—a king plus a board pair—to make the nut full house. And even then, he would be hoping that no one makes quads when the board pairs. He also could win with two running spades, one of which would need to be the ace, to make the nut flush. See why he instinctively gets worried with this type of hand combined with this kind of flop?

When you hold cards that will make the nut flush, and the flop comes with two or three of your suit, you are in position to drive. However, be cautious in pushing a second-nut flush. The number of king-high flushes beaten by ace-high flushes seems to be astronomical in Omaha high-low. The check-call may be your best alternative with a second-nut flush when you are in a front position, if you choose to continue with it at all.

If the board shows either a high card (preferably the highest rank on board) that matches your pocket pair, or a pair that matches one of the ranks in your hand, again you show potential for a winning result, provided your trips are not the lowest possible.

If the flop shows three unrelated cards, there is often very little action when it hits. In that case, if you hold any promise for either a low or high draw, you can continue to play. But unless you flop trips, your best strategy is usually to wait and see. When I say "wait and see," I mean that you call someone's bet or you check in the hopes of getting to see a free card on the next street.

2. MAKING THE SECOND NUTS

Suppose you hold this hand:

The flop comes:

Ask yourself, "If I make the flush, how likely is it that I will win the pot?" Less-than-nut flushes, unless they are backdoor flushes, are legendary for biting the dust in Omaha high-low. What do I mean by making a "backdoor" flush? Making a **backdoor hand** is just another way of saying that you caught cards on fourth and fifth streets to make a hand that you weren't drawing to on the flop. In the example above, if an opponent were holding a hand with two medium clubs in it and caught a club on the turn and river, his flush wouldn't necessarily need to be the best-possible flush to win the pot. Why? Because no one probably would be drawing against him with only one club showing on the flop.

Just as dangerous as making the **third-nut** (third-best possible) flush is making the **second-nut** (second-best possible) straight because it is often harder to get away from. If you don't have the potential to make the top straight, even if you flop the temporary nuts, you are in danger. It is not unusual for a straight to be counterfeited in Omaha high-low, especially if you flop it. As demonstrated in the previous hand example, many seasoned players will not bet a straight aggressively until the river unless they have other draws to go with it. This concept goes against the grain of many converted hold'em players who play straights aggressively.

Another danger in second nutsmanship is flopping the middle or low set (three of a kind) when there are higher ranks on the flop. Nothing can be more demoralizing than making the second-nut or even third-nut full house. In a $4/$8 Omaha high-low game that I played in a tiny little cardroom somewhere in northern California, this scenario took place:

THE FLOP

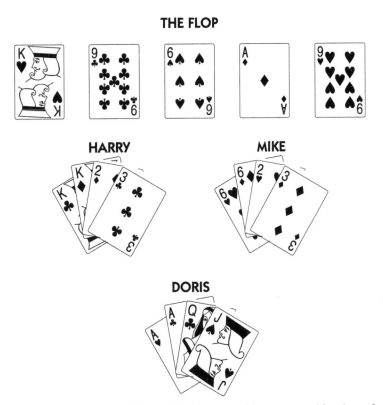

Harry flopped top set (kings), Mike flopped bottom set (sixes), and Doris flopped an inside straight draw with an overpair (aces). The turn showed an ace, giving Doris top set. When nines paired on the river, Harry thought he had the winning hand and lost a $200 pot with kings full, the second-nut full house.

Hooked into the betting with his lowest possible full house, Mike left the table moaning about a bad beat. But was it a bad beat or simply bad judgment? Sitting in a late position, he had called the preflop action with a weak hand. When Harry bet into him on the flop, he could have thrown in a comparatively inexpensive raise to probe the strength of his opponent's hand. Doris would probably have reraised, at which point Mike could have dumped his hand without further loss. Maybe Mike was one of those optimistic losers I mentioned earlier in the book.

3. PLAYING THE WHEEL

When your nut-low hand is the wheel with no better hand possible on the board, be aggressive with your betting, even if you know that someone else also has a wheel—the two of you will split the pot anyway. But if a 6-high or 7-high straight is possible and you believe that another player has made it, play conservatively if you also believe that you and the third player both have the wheel and will get quartered by the higher straight. Take a look at the following scenario, which pictures a fairly common situation with low hands:

THE FLOP

DORA

RICHARD

HOMER

Both Homer and Dora have wheels, and Homer also has a 6-high straight. Richard holds both a wheel and the nut 7-high straight. With $300 in the pot, Richard will win one-half of it for the high straight ($150), and another one-third of the low half of the pot. Homer, who also has a wheel and a 6-high straight, and Dora will each receive only one-sixth of the total pot ($50 each), giving them a return of minus 50 percent on their investment.

Suppose you're involved in one of those rare low-limit pots where there are only two of you at the river. Each of you has made the wheel. If the 5-4-3 are among the common cards, your opponent will win three-quarters of the pot if he holds the A-K-6-2, for example, and you have only the A-2. Consider these kinds of possibilities in playing your wheel hands.

For instance, if you are fairly certain (based on the past betting) that your opponent has a wheel, you may wish to check your hand to him if you are first to bet. If you are second to bet, it is usually wise to simply smooth-call if you do not possess 2-6 or 6-7 along with your wheel.

If you bet first and your opponent raises, usually do not reraise with anything less than the A-2-6. Call only, for he is quite likely to hold the A-2-6 and perhaps even the A-2-6-7, in which case you will win only one-quarter of the pot.

4. SECOND-NUT HIGH

Whether you should call with the second-nut high at the river depends upon the betting. If there have been no raises and if the driver (an aggressive player who is dominating the betting) checks, you may feel safe in wagering on your second-nut high hand. But if the driver continues his thrust, you are in danger of losing your bet if you call.

There are some circumstances, however, when you can bet or call with the second-nut high:

a. The board suddenly changes its character on fifth street.

For example, two running suited cards appear on the turn and river making a flush possible. You believe that the former driver has been betting his straight and you have made a medium-high flush. If he again bets, call only, but if he checks, take the initiative and bet.

b. The driver is a known bluffer and you believe that your hand is at least equal to his.

Actually, players do occasionally bluff in low-limit Omaha high-low, though it is about as rare as everyone folding to the big blind before the flop.

c. The driver is sitting in last position and either a threatening or a disappointing card appears at the river.

A threat may be a third suited card or a board pair. A disappointment could be no third flush or straight card. If you suspect that the driver was on a draw that is different from what the board shows at the river, you may call his bet with a reasonable hand. If he had been drawing on the come to a busted flush, your two pair may turn out to be the best high hand.

Suppose you have been the aggressor pushing with your nut straight. The board either pairs or a third flush card comes on the river. Be prepared to sink in its muddy waters (fold!) if an entirely new bettor initiates the wagering. He probably has made his flush or full house and your nut straight is toast.

Players who have difficulty releasing a hand that probably has been beaten on the river lose unnecessary chips by calling end bets too often. It is especially tough to fold an ace-high flush. But when the board pairs on the river, making a full house possible for an opponent, you usually should fold your flush if:

a. Someone you think has been betting a high hand all along bets right into you;

b. You bet and he raises behind you; or

c. One player bets, another raises, and a third opponent reraises before it's your turn to bet.

You don't want to get whiplashed, caught between a couple of low hands and an opponent who has just overtaken your flush by making a better high.

5. SECOND-NUT LOW

More players have probably lost end bets with the second-nut low than with almost any other holding in low-limit Omaha high-low. I hate the second-nut low more than any other thing I can think of in high-low poker. Especially annoying is Tight Ted who has checked his nut low from the flop onward, leaving aggression to the high hands and deceiving you into believing that no one has the nut low.

If you have good reason to believe that someone has the nut low at the river, fold your hand even if it was the best low until the final moment of truth. If a new bettor, who is not the one who has been driving with the probable high hand, bets when a deuce falls on the river, fold your A-2-4 because you probably are beaten by A-2-3. This is especially true if the new bettor is someone like Lowball Larry, who usually plays nothing but A-2 with two backup cards to the wheel.

But there's good news, too. If no one appears to have a good low, yours probably is the best one available and you stand to win half the pot with it. This sometimes happens when the ubiquitous deuce falls on the river and the suspected nut-low holder suddenly checks. Now your A-4 is looking very strong. You can bet it, provided no one else that you suspect of having the nut low bets into you, and the only other bettor is the person that you've put on the nut high. In tracing the betting, if it appears that no one has ever pretended to have the nut low, and if you have the second nuts, you can probably feel safe in betting or calling with it on the river.

9. HOW TO WIN LOW-LIMIT POKER TOURNAMENTS

THE BASICS OF TOURNAMENT PLAY

Casinos and Internet poker rooms offer several types of tournaments. Most low-limit casino tournaments are rebuy events. In a **rebuy tournament** you can buy more chips during the first three levels of play and you can make one final rebuy (an **add-on**) at the end of the rebuy period. Most high-stakes tournaments are freezeout events. In a **freezeout tournament**, you cannot buy more chips. When you have lost your starting stack of chips, you must give up your seat in the tournament.

Another type of tournament is a **satellite**, a preliminary tournament that you can play to earn an entry into the main event. Satellites cost much less to enter than the main event and are an inexpensive way to buy in to a tournament that has a big entry fee. Most players who enter the World Series of Poker $10,000 championship tournament earn their buy-ins by winning a satellite that costs from $40 up to $1,000.

Whereas cash games are designed to keep players in the game, tournaments are designed to knock them out of the game. The purpose of a tournament is to eliminate contestants until only one player has won all the chips. Unlike cash games in which the blinds remain the same throughout the duration of the game, the blinds increase at regular intervals during a tournament. Each interval is called a **level**, during which the blinds remain constant for 20 minutes, 30 minutes, an hour, or whatever time frame the tournament sponsor has designated. When a new level begins, the blinds increase by 50 percent up to 100 percent, depending upon the design of the tournament. But one thing's for sure: If you never play a hand, you will eventually go broke just from paying the two blind bets that you are forced to post during each round of play.

The design of a tournament is referred to as its **structure**. A tournament's structure includes such factors as the number of chips each player receives at the start of the event, the size of the blinds at the start of the tournament, whether rebuys are allowed, the length of each level, and the percentage of increase in the blinds from one level to the next. Some tournaments are structured to end quickly. For example, satellites are fast-moving tournament events. Other tournaments, such as the World Series of Poker, World Poker Tour events, and the championship event in other major tournaments are structured to last a long time and give players plenty of time to play.

ASSESSING A TOURNMAENT

Before you enter a tournament, ask the following 11 questions. The answers will help you design your tournament strategy.

1. How much is the buy-in?

The buy-in is often $20 to $40 for low-limit casino tournaments. In addition to that, the casino usually charges an entry fee to cover the house expenses for running the tournament. The usual entry fee in low-limit tournaments is about 15 to 20 percent of the buy-in. Sometimes the entry fee is included in the buy-in amount and is simply subtracted from the total prize pool of the tournament.

2. Is this tournament a rebuy event or a freezeout?
If you're playing a freezeout event, you need only the amount of the entry fee plus the vig. If you're playing a rebuy tournament, bring enough money with you to make several rebuys and an add-on.

3. How much do rebuys and add-ons cost, and when can I make them?
Any time you have fewer chips in your stack than you had in your starting stack, you can buy more chips, but only for a limited time. You usually can rebuy only during the first three rounds of play (the rebuy period). At the end of the rebuy period, most rebuy events allow you to buy additional tournament chips (an add-on) for the same price you would pay for a rebuy.

4. What is the usual prize pool?
The size of the prize pool is determined by the number of entries. Tournament directors keep records and can tell you the average amount of money that the winner usually wins. I always like to know how much I will earn if I win so that I can keep my "eyes on the prize," as the old saying goes.

5. How many places are paid?
The number of players who get paid usually depends on the number of entries. Small daily tournaments in hometown cardrooms might pay only the final three players, while others reward the last five players in action. Tournaments with 100 entries usually pay everyone at the last table, and larger events pay two or more tables.

6. What percentage of the prize pool does each finalist receive?
The winning player usually gets 37 to 40 percent of the prize pool, with second place earning 20 to 25 percent and the remaining finalists dividing the rest of the money.

7. How long are the betting rounds?
In the majority of low-limit tourneys, the betting rounds are 20 minutes long, with a 15-minute break after the first hour of play.

8. How many chips will I receive to start with?
The lower the amount of the buy-in, the fewer chips you usually receive in your starting stack. If you enter a $20 buy-in event, you often will be given $200 in tournament chips. In a $1,000 buy-in tournament, you might start with $2,000 in chips.

9. What are the blinds in the first round of play?
In a low-limit tournament, the blinds often begin at $5/$10. The amount of the blinds in relation to the size of your starting stack of chips is an important indicator of how much "play" you will get for your money. Usually you want to receive at least 10 times the size of the big blind in your starting stack of chips.

10. How early should I be there to sign up?
Ask the tournament director in advance when tournament registration begins and whether he cuts it off at either a certain hour or after a designated number of players have paid their entry fees. I recommend arriving one hour before starting time for a Las Vegas tournament.

11. Which side games does the cardroom spread?
If you wash out of the tournament early, you'll probably want to play a cash game at which you excel. Be sure that the cardroom spreads your game of choice.

Now that you know the basics of tournaments, here are some guidelines for how to select the best tournaments to play. First, making a good choice means playing within your bankroll and comfort zone. Don't gamble with the rent money playing a tournament that is too expensive for your budget. Second, you need to reserve the proper time commitment. Figure out how long it will take to play the tournament if you get to the final table and, hopefully, win it. Make sure that you can be there mentally as well as physically for the duration of the tournament. If you will need to be somewhere else during the maximum length of time you think the tournament will require, skip that day's event, because your heart very likely will not be in it.

I play a lot of tournaments in casinos year around. Since I can't be everywhere at once, I choose the events that I most want to play and mark them on my calendar. It is okay to schedule new games on your calendar, too, but just make sure that the cost of learning to play an unfamiliar tournament game is not too expensive. In other words, start small and work your way up if you like the game and are having some success with it.

10 WINNING TIPS FOR TOURNAMENT PLAY

WINNING TIP #1
Play Straightforward Poker in Low-limit Tournaments

The value of deception decreases in low-limit tournament play for several reasons. First, many players, especially new ones, do not pay attention to their opponents. Therefore any deceptive plays you try probably will go right past them. For example, suppose you've been playing tight as a drum and decide to take advantage of your tight table image by raising under the gun with a mediocre hand. Your bluff probably will backfire because most of your opponents are oblivious to the fact that you haven't played a hand for a long time. Second, the players at your table change frequently as people go broke and are replaced by new opponents. There is an inverse ratio between deceptive value and the number of times players are rotated to your table. Many times, too, your table will be broken down and you will move to another table with all new opponents.

Slowplaying your solid hands in order to get more value for them usually is not a good idea in low buy-in tournaments. Why? Because the pace is fast and you usually will get plenty of callers even if you bet a good hand strongly, especially in the early rounds when most of your opponents are playing loose poker. Continue playing solid poker throughout the tournament rather than falling into the trap of playing loose just because you can rebuy if you go broke. You do not have to be a maniac to win a tournament. Sure, maniacs will win once in a while, but it is usually the solid, selectively aggressive players who wind up in the winners' circle.

Remember that most of the players in a low buy-in event are neither highly skilled nor very experienced. Therefore some of the bluffs and fancy plays that might work against better opponents will fall flat against beginners.

WINNING TIP #2
Play Small Tournaments at First
Very few players have the bankroll or the ability to be competitive in the big buy-in tournaments without first playing in the smaller ones. People who skip the smaller tournaments and go directly for the World Series of Poker or the World Poker Tour events are seldom successful to start with. It takes lots of experience and practice to acquire the skills you need to compete on a level playing field with some of the best tournament players in the world. Fortunately, there are many small buy-in tournaments available both online and

> *Don Gay*
> "*Anticipation—wanting to get there—caused him to lose the bull.*"
> *World Champion Bull Rider*

in brick-and-mortar casinos to choose from where you can practice and improve your tournament skills.

Playing in low buy-in tournaments can be a very inexpensive way to get the experience needed to move up the tournament ladder. If you are successful and make money at the smaller buy-in events, you are usually ready to play in bigger events and face tougher competition. Most of us rise to the level of our competition. Nobody in sports improves his performance by always competing against players of lesser ability. On the other hand, you can lose a lot of money by playing in tournaments where the competition is too tough for you.

So what's the answer? I personally believe that playing in small buy-in tournaments online is the way to go. Online tournaments in every poker game imaginable are usually available around the clock. If you keep good records of your wins and losses, you will know when it's time to move up. When your winning record over six months, for example, far exceeds your losses, try moving to a higher buy-in tournament where the competition is stiffer. Give the bigger buy-in tournaments two or three shots. If you feel comfortable competing at that level and believe you can become a winner, stay there for a while. Then move up to an ever higher rung on the tournament ladder. But if you get slaughtered every time you put your buy-in on the butcher block, step back down the ladder until you have more experience and expertise under your belt.

WINNING TIP #3
Play the Player as Well as Your Cards

Some players believe that their toughest opponents at the tournament table are players like Phil or T.J. or Annie—you know, the seasoned champions with bracelets up to their elbows—but that isn't always the case. Meek Marvin can cause you just as much trouble in a tournament as Maniac Mike. Sometimes it's that passive limper sitting in seat eight who causes you the most head-aches.

What *do* you do when you're playing in a tournament against a loose passive player who plays a lot of hands, calls raises with marginal cards, *and* has a lot of chips? You simply have to wait for a better starting hand with which to attack him. You can't afford to mix it up with marginal starting hands against this type of guy because he is virtually bluff-proof. Occasionally however, I'll be so short-stacked that I simply must play a marginal hand against this type of player and hope that it wins.

You are correct in feeling unhappy about committing a significant portion of your chips in these types of situations. These players are always dangerous when they have lots of chips because they are unpredictable. When you're in a multiway pot with them, they are less of a factor because you're not fighting them alone. Meek Marvin is especially dangerous shorthanded when you're trying to isolate against only one other player because he keeps calling and getting in your way, in contrast to Maniac Mike who keeps raising and getting in the way. Eventually both types usually self-destruct.

Remember that you have to play the player just as much as you play your hand, particularly in no-limit hold'em. One way to handle a wild player is to come over the top of him. Another way to handle a maniac is to simply get out of his way.

WINNING TIP #4
Design a Tournament Strategy
Like automobiles, tournaments come in many shapes and sizes. Depending on whether you like to drive in the slow lane or prefer the fast lane, you can play small tournaments with $20 buy-ins or less in casinos across the country any day of the week and 24-7 on the Internet—or you can take a shot at the granddaddy of them all by dragging $10,000 out of your pocket for a buy-in to the

World Series of Poker. And if you really want to live large, you can get a second mortgage on your home to post the $25,000 buy-in for the championship event of the World Poker Tour. No matter what size tournament you enter, plan your strategy in advance as a sort of road map for your journey through the rounds of the tournament.

Most of the larger buy-in tournaments are freeze-out events that don't allow you to buy more chips when you go broke. If you lose all your chips, you're out of action. Rebuy tournaments give you a second chance when you lose your stack. Most of the smaller tournaments—those with buy-ins of $20 to $100—allow you to rebuy for the first three rounds of the tournament and make one more rebuy (an add-on) at the end of the third round. Freeze-out tournaments and rebuy events require somewhat different strategies. Generally speaking, you should play more conservatively in freeze-out tournaments, especially in the early rounds, than you play in rebuy events. Most top players play very solid poker in freeze-out tournaments, entering pots only when they have good hands and are in good table position.

In rebuy tournaments, players usually play more loosely during the rebuy period (the first three rounds) than they do after the rebuy period has ended. At the end of the rebuy period, you'll often hear seasoned players say, "Now the real tournament begins!" In other words, people play more solid poker when they know they can't buy more chips. Before you enter a rebuy event, you should decide how many rebuys you can afford and the conditions under which you will make them. For example, if you budget three rebuys and an add-on in a $20 rebuy tournament ($100 total), your strategy might include going all-in if you need to, rebuying if you lose that all-in pot, and adding on at the end of the rebuy period if weak players have the tall stacks. The key is to plan your tournament strategy in advance—aggressive early, survival late, attack the short stacks, lay back with a low stack, and so forth. Write your plan on the back of a business card and take it with you. Then stick with the plan for as long as it works for you.

"I recall reading that it is best to accumulate chips early in a tournament by being a little more aggressive," Ken, who plays a lot of low-limit casino poker tournaments, said in his e-mail. "But late in the tournament, I've read that you should play much tighter and let the other players knock each other out, provided that the blinds aren't eating you up. What's your opinion?"

Yes, you want to increase your stack in the early rounds, but not at the risk of either busting out or investing more money on rebuys than the tournament is worth. It's always a dilemma, so I usually gauge my number of rebuys according to the size of the tournament and how the cards are running for me. If I'm running bad, I run for the door real early.

But if you're playing in a freeze-out tournament, I suggest following the advice of Linda Johnson, spokesperson for the World Poker Tour. "What does it take to get the money? When I first started playing, I played much tighter than I do now. Then I came to realize that you have to accumulate chips early. If you don't have them when the limits go up, you're in trouble. You might play a few more "button" hands, especially in Texas hold'em tournaments. Plus, a few more marginal hands in the beginning that I never would have played in a tournament years ago.

"What you have to remember in tournament play is that in the beginning, you can see a flop for, say, $20, but in two hours that flop is going to cost you $100. So you can see five flops now for the same price as one flop later on. You can lose all five $20 flops and still have some money left, but if you hit a few of them you'll have a lot of chips. I would rather play J-10 five times early on hoping to get lucky than wait for aces once, because I can't play that J-10 when the limits get very high. It gets to the point where you can't play those marginal hands because they cost you too much."

Linda is right. Here's what happens: In the beginning stage of the tournament, there are more multiway pots so you can come in with hands such as J-10 or 9-8 suited. But in the later stages it's almost "raise or release." You're playing that J-10 against one or two people at the most who already have brought the pot in for a raise, so you couldn't possibly have the best hand. Your J-10 is totally unplayable because you aren't getting the right price for it.

WINNING TIP #5
Use Good Judgment in Deciding Whether to Rebuy and Add On

Enter a rebuy tournament with enough money to make rebuys and the optional add-on. Some players plan to fire just one bullet—they intend to stick with their original buy-in only and quit if they lose it. This puts them at a disadvantage to their opponents who are willing to rebuy. In most rebuy events, you will need to take advantage of the rebuy or add-on options to get to the final table. Your chip position, your budget, and the strength of the players who are in top chips status are determining factors in deciding whether you should add on at the end of the rebuy period. If the casino awards bonus chips in addition to the usual number of chips you would receive when you add on, you are almost always correct in taking the add-on. Or if buying the add-on will increase your chip position by 33 percent or more, take the add-on.

Should you plan to always rebuy when you go broke? Not necessarily. If I get broke late in the rebuy period just after the limits have risen, I will often quit rather than go for another rebuy. Why? Because the amount of chips that I will receive for my rebuy money is much smaller in relation to the higher limits. For example, if I will receive $200 in chips for the rebuy when the blinds are $25/$50, those chips won't go nearly as far as they would have gone when the blinds were only $10/$20 in an earlier round. The bottom line is to use good judgment in your rebuy decisions. Ask yourself, "Will a rebuy at this stage of the tournament under these conditions be a good investment?"

WINNING TIP #6
Play More Conservatively in Freeze-out Tournaments

In freeze-out tournaments, in which no rebuys are allowed, you are frozen out of action when you run out of chips. You must survive with your original stack of chips and build it along the way if you are to have any hope of winning. Since the opening limits and blinds are fairly small in relation to the chips in play, I recommend a more conservative strategy during the early rounds of play.

One of the best pieces of tournament advice—for which Tom McEvoy has been quoted numerous times in poker literature—is this: "You must survive long enough in the tournament to give yourself a chance to get lucky."

What does it mean?

Nobody ever won a tournament without getting lucky at some point. Getting lucky could mean that you made a flush when your opponent flopped trips, or that you had aces when another player had kings. Or maybe your opponents missed their drawing hands and you won the pot with a low pair. No matter how it happens, you can't get lucky if you're not in it. And that is why I believe that knowing how to survive is such an important skill.

Survival skills are necessary to win, but learning these skills takes time and practice, plus a whole lot of patience. It isn't much fun to fold hand after hand, is it? Waiting for the cards to turn in my favor, or waiting for the correct moment to make a play is not my idea of having a good time at the poker table. But as the old saying goes, "You gotta do what you gotta do."

Oftentimes you see players make very reckless bets and raises, and play cards you would never dream of playing. Sometimes they get lucky for a while, but most of the time they crash and burn, usually sooner rather than later. If these rammer-jammers do survive with large stacks of chips, they often forget that they need to slow down and preserve them. That's when they find out the hard way that they can lose them just as fast as they won them. There's no need for you to have to learn that lesson on your own—learn from their bad example and continue playing good poker all the way.

WINNING TIP #7
Keep Track of Your Stack

Always be aware of your stack's status relative to the size of your opponents' stacks, and your playing position at the table. For example, if you have a very low stack with an average hand in middle position, be more inclined to throw away your hand. Save your dwindling chips for a stronger hand in a later, more favorable playing position.

When you're in a strong chip status and good position at the table, play opportunistically—attack small stacks with a raise when you have a playable hand, especially against very tight players. And late in the tournament, especially at the final table, use your big stack as a weapon of mass destruction.

If your stack resembles a molehill rather than the Matterhorn, you are often well advised to use survival tactics, rather than going up against a tall stack that could knock you out of the tournament.

WINNING TIP #8
Watch the Clock

Many tournaments have a tournament clock somewhere in the room. This clock tells you what the current limits are, what time the next increase in limits will take place, and how much time is left in the round. It often will also note how many players started the tournament and how many are still left. Sometimes the clock will determine your strategy, just like it does in a football game. With 45 seconds remaining in the first half, a team might try an onside kick designed to steal the football from the enemy. Similarly, with only two minutes left in the betting round, you might raise from the button with a medium-strength hand to try to steal the blinds or build the pot, hoping that other players call and you get lucky on the flop.

Think of the tournament as an apple pie that is divided into as many pieces as there are betting rounds. You sometimes need to time your moves according to the number of remaining pieces in the pie. When you are in favorable position late in the betting round, for example, you may decide to play a reasonable drawing hand more aggressively than you would otherwise play it. Why? Because the betting limits will double within the next two hands, making such a draw twice as expensive to take.

"If you can win one pot at each increment, you can sustain yourself," advised "Bulldog" Sykes, whose low-limit tournament winning record was exemplary.

WINNING TIP #9
Get Smart Late
Late in a tournament, you cannot always wait for a premium hand because the antes and blinds begin gobbling up your chips like Pac Man. Neither can you afford to take high-risk draws or play aggressively to try to get maximum value for your hand.

Whether a play is smart or not-so-smart depends on four things:

1. The strength of your hand;
2. Your comparative chip status;
3. The nature of your opponents;
4. Your philosophy about whether it is more important to arrive at the final table, even with minimal chips, or whether it is better to gamble with your short stack in an attempt to build up your stack for a better shot at the tournament's bulls-eye.

You can't wait for the nuts or even a big hand. You have to take a shot with any playable hand and be aggressive with it. Not everybody agrees with me, of course. Some tournament aficionados advise more conservative play, using survival tactics to arrive at the final table rather than risking taking a dive out of the tournament's money pool. I prefer to play conservatively at the next-to-last table, for example, no matter what the size of my stack, because I love competing at the final table and believe that if I can just make it that far, I'll have a shot at the brass ring.

WINNING TIP #10
Keep Your Cool Under Pressure

The biggest tournament mistake a player can make is giving up hope. "I have won hundreds of tournaments during my 25-year career as a tournament specialist—including the World Series of Poker championship—but I have never won a tournament without being in what looked like a hopeless chip position sometime during the event," 1983 World Champion of Poker Tom McEvoy told me. "I waited for what I thought was the best hand or the best situation to put my last few chips in the pot. And I never gave up hope."

Don't throw your last chip in the pot simply out of desperation or frustration. Don't let other players distract you, or allow lady luck to demoralize you. After all, this is the only chance you'll ever get to win this tournament, today, right now.

Winston Churchill put it this way: "Never ever, ever, ever give up!" I wonder if he played poker?

BONUS WINNING TIP
Shane's C.O.R.E. Approach to Tournaments

Tournament poker is a game of mistakes. So often, you can play perfect tournament strategy deep into the tournament, then make one or two mistakes, and be forced to head for the rail rather than the roses. C.O.R.E.—Concentrate, Observe, Remember, and Execute—is an acronym for my approach to both tournaments and cash games. It should help you avoid getting stuck by the thorns on your poker roses.

Concentrate

Keep your eyes on the prize every second of the time you're playing in a tournament. Don't let distractions obstruct your vision of victory. Remain in the moment, fully focused on the challenges at hand.

Observe

T.J. Cloutier is famous for saying that if a wing fell off a gnat at the opposite end of the poker table, he would see it flutter to the felt. He uses that comment to illustrate the importance of observing your opponents, getting to know their playing habits, and picking up their tells.

Remember

Perhaps the greatest poker champion of all time, Doyle Brunson, lists "recall" as one the most important traits of winning players. Both he and T.J. claim that after playing poker with someone once, they can recall that player's habits the next time they meet, even if it is years later.

Execute

You've maintained your concentration and discipline. Nothing has escaped your powers of observation. You remember how your opponents have played most of their hands. But none of that knowledge is useful until you use it to your advantage. You are not a poker scholar who simply learns and stores knowledge like an encyclopedia. You are a player who knows what to do, how to do it, who to do it to, and who not to mess with. Now it's time to perform. Using your reservoir of knowledge and skills, you move into action and execute your game plan with confidence. You are a winner!

A FINAL WORD FROM P.C.

"Shane, with the World Series of Poker right around the corner and top players from around the world in town, I'm glad you're winding up your diver-to-thriver stuff with these timely tournament tips. At last you've advanced from the ho-hum vanilla of cash games to the Bavarian chocolate of tournaments. But why didn't you write more about specific tournament strategies?" my poker conscience nags.

"P.C.," I fire back, "you've got a good point, but I figure that this advice is enough to get anyone started off on the right track, and serious players who want more in-depth advice will invest a few extra bucks in McEvoy and Vines' book, *How to Win No-Limit Hold'em Tournaments* or my other book, *Poker Tournament Tips from the Pros*. Until we talk again, P.C., please tell my flirtatious friend, Lady Luck, that Shane needs her at the final table."

With that, P.C. retreats to contemplate my request.

You need to continually be aware of the size of your stack in proportion to the size of your opponents' stacks, and what round of the tournament you are in. In the early to middle rounds, chips begin to get redistributed and you need to know who has the bigger stacks and who has the smaller stacks, and where your stack stands in relationship to theirs.
—*Tom McEvoy in* Tournament Poker

Near the end of a tournament there aren't enough good hands to go around in the fast rounds that are left to play. So who gets the money? The Foxes do. They know how to steal; they know when to go with less than perfect starts; and they recognize opportunities when they see them. Foxes are very clever—and they win the money. You need to know how and when to play like a Fox.
—*D. R. Sherer*

10. WINNING TOURNAMENT ADVICE

The advice in this section was written in collaboration with my former writing partners Tom McEvoy and Don Vines. We always enjoyed pooling our wits and wisdom to come up with new approaches to familiar poker subjects. My primary job was to create a suitable outline, tape Tom and Don's knowledge and expertise, and then transform their impeccable grasp of poker skills into informative and entertaining magazine articles for *Player* magazine, by our mutual publisher, Avery Cardoza. I sincerely hope you gain a great deal of added knowledge from the fruits of our mutual efforts on how to win hold'em tournaments of all types.

WHAT'S YOUR GAME PLAN FOR WINNING?

By Don Vines

Don Gay

"You've to figure out your game plan when you draw a bull like that."

World Champion Bull Rider

Just like a football team follows a game plan that is tailored to beat each team it plays, you need to design a personal game plan for winning no-limit hold'em tournaments.

Here is a sample game plan that you can modify to suit your own style of play. If you plan your play, and then play your plan, we're sure to meet at the championship table some time soon.

LEARN YOUR OPPONENTS
Start off by putting your opponents into four slots: loose, tight, overly aggressive, and solid aggressive. Notice how they bet their hands. Are they prone to overbet or underbet? Do they bluff? And most importantly, do they protect their blinds?

PLAY YOUR POSITION
Play solid no-limit hold'em in front positions, but loosen up your starting hand requirements when you're sitting on the backside. For example, if a couple of players have limped into the pot, you can call with a wide range of hands you wouldn't play from up front—A-J, K-Q, Q-10, J-10, almost any pair, and suited connectors no lower than 6-5.

PLAY A PATIENT GAME
Wait for the right cards in the right position. Don't panic if you don't have any playable hands for what seems like an eternity. The cards will come, sometimes sooner, sometimes later. Patience and discipline are the keys to winning. In a tournament with 20-minute levels, expect to get one good hand to play in each level. With 30-minute levels, you should get two playable hands. I've played in tournaments where I didn't play a hand for two levels, and yet I still made it to the championship table.

PLAY THE STACK SIZES
Always be aware of the stack size of your opponents, because your stack size relative to theirs can determine your action against them. Don't attack a player who has chips equal to or larger than your stack size unless you have the nuts. Try to put the small stacks under pressure—give them some heat under which they may make

mistakes. If they're wrong, they're out and their chips end up in your stack.

DEVELOP A TABLE PRESENCE

Establish yourself as a "player" by always playing your best game and keeping pressure on your opponents. Establish your own standards about how much to raise rather than following the pack. And show them that you know how to make great folds when you sense that you're beaten.

SWITCH GEARS

Sometimes change your style of play to keep your opponents off balance. After establishing your image as a solid-aggressive player who only raises with premium hands, for example, switch gears to the loose-aggressive mode by raising a few pots in a row. Chances are good that you'll pick up a pot or two. But if you get played with and have to show a mediocre hand, switch back to solid-aggressive play.

USE POKER MATH

Know the percentages regarding whether your hand is a favorite or an underdog by calculating your pot odds for winning or losing. Tailor the size of your bets in tricky situations to avoid giving your opponents the right odds to call. Overbetting the pot may be just the invitation they need to call you.

PLAY SMART IN THE BLIND

Always remember that once you post the small blind or big blind, the money you've shoved into the middle no longer is yours. It belongs to the pot, not you. Every time you call a raise from either of the blinds, you will be out of position from the flop onward. Therefore only protect your blind when you have a premium hand.

OCCASIONALLY BLUFF

The bluff is a sharp tool you can use to build your chips in no-limit hold'em tournaments. You cannot win a tournament by just playing the cards you are dealt, because in the short run, you usually are not dealt enough good hands to go all the way. Use the total bluff in late position when the only way you can win is by betting. Use the semi-bluff in situations where you don't have the best hand at the moment, but it can improve to the best hand if the right card comes off on the turn or river.

ALWAYS PLAY YOUR A-GAME

Today's big-field tournaments are tougher than ever to beat. Top players turn out when the big money is on the line—and to beat them, you must play your best poker every minute you're at the table. Work these six tips into your A-Game plan:

1. If an opponent is on a rush, get out of his way. Wait until his rush is over before you try to run over him.

2. Don't try to bluff a loose player. It is beneath the dignity of some players to fold. In the trade, we refer to them as "idiots." You do not want to make idiot-bluffs against them.

3. Try to get full value out of your good hands by Value betting. That is, bet an amount that you believe your opponent will call so that you can win a bigger pot.

4. Don't play "sheriff." A sheriff will call a bet on the end just to let his opponent know that he can't get away with

stealing the pot in case he doesn't have the winning hand. Sheriffs fall into the trap of putting their opponent on a hand they can beat just to justify calling. Before calling a bet, always consider the number of hands you cannot beat rather than the one hand you can beat.

5. Don't play when you're tired at the start of the tournament. Or when you are not willing to long hours. And especially don't play when you are not fully committed to playing your A-Game.

6. Finally, don't let losing upset you. Realize that you will lose a lot more tournaments than you will win. When you do win, the pride, the exhilaration, and the money more than make up for all the times you lost. Indeed winning cures a lot of ills.

THE 7 SUCCESS STRATEGIES OF GREAT TOURNAMENT PLAYERS

By Tom McEvoy & Don Vines

Wanna join the ranks of the great poker players atop the tournament totem pole? Try practicing these seven success strategies that have taken poker greats such as Doyle Brunson, T.J. Cloutier and Johnny Chan to the top of the heap. Not only is imitation the ultimate compliment, it is the most practical way to move your game upward to the highest level.

READ BETWEEN THE LINES

Great no-limit hold'em players spend many hours studying other players, fine-tuning their ability to put their opponents on a certain hand before the flop. But they are always willing to change their initial analysis after the flop, on the turn, and even on the river, when they sense that the situation has changed. Great players also know how to evaluate the strength of their hand versus your hand by expertly reading the significance of the board cards. And whether they are active in a hand or not, poker pros constantly analyze the play of hands as to who did what in which situations, chalking it all up on the blackboard in their mind. If you want to join their ranks, we suggest that you continually practice reading between the lines to improve your game.

KNOW THE MATHEMATICS OF BIG-BET POKER

It isn't enough to be a great reader if you don't know the math and how to apply it to different situations. Expert players may not be academically trained mathematicians (though some of them are), but they understand the odds and how to apply them either in betting, calling or raising. Great players are able to fold even the best starting hands when the pot odds are not in their favor. Watching televised poker events, you've probably heard the program's host say, "What a great laydown! Doyle would've lost all his chips if he had called Johnny's all-in bet." But they also are able to shove in a mountain of chips when they calculate that they have the best of it. Math and poker walk hand in hand along the trail to tournament victory.

LEARN HOW MUCH TO BET

The best players know how much to bet when they want you to call. And they have a feel for how much to bet if they want you to lay down a hand. They are expert at Value betting in order to increase the probability of being called. When you see great players take their time before betting, they are reviewing the hand and deciding how much to bet. Like topnotch salespeople, they are experts at selling a hand. Essentially, they put a price on a hand that they believe you're willing to buy, and then announce the sales tag to you with their bet or raise.

STAY ON TARGET AND OFF TILT

Great players are even-tempered at the table. They have the ability to shrug off bad beats without throwing their games off track by beating themselves up if they misplay a hand. They may go for a walk to regain their composure or they may just laugh it off, but they get back into the great-player mode very quickly. And yes, even Phil Hellmuth, known for his tantrums at the table, shifts his game back into gear as soon as he's blown off some steam.

ADJUST YOUR PLAY

In poker parlance, we call adjusting your play to the current conditions of the game "maneuvering." Champions know how to maneuver—play fast, slow down, accelerate, coast—according to their chip position and the current playing styles of their opponents at any time during a tournament. Their ultimate goal is always to win the tournament—or to at least make it to the final three players at the championship table because they know that's where the big money is—and they pull every trick they have out of their tournament bag to reach that goal.

CONSTANTLY EVALUATE YOUR GAME

Top players have the ability to recognize their own weaknesses, and are willing to work on them in order to improve their game so that they become even better players. They are true students of the game and are always open to plugging their leaks and learning new things. "I enjoy the challenge of playing with the best," Jennifer Harmon Traniello said in *Poker Aces*. "It's a constant learning experience. I make mistakes, but as long as I learn something from those mistakes, they can actually be good for me."

"Poker is like sex. We all have a certain natural ability, but it takes practice to get good."

John Vorhaus, poker author

A lot of pros talk over the play of hands with their peers, away from the tables of course. Go into think-tank mode with your most trusted poker buddies, keeping the focus on how to improve your play, and you'll reap the benefits of thinking outside the box.

ACCEPT VICTORY OR DEFEAT WITH CLASS

True champions are gracious in victory or defeat. When they get lucky and put a beat on another player, you'll hear them say something like, "I sure got lucky on that one." And if another player puts a beat on them, they don't bemoan their fate or go ballistic and berate their opponent's play. Nor are they exhibitionists at the table.

When you win, someone else loses. Losers feel bad, especially when they lose a big pot at a crucial time in a tournament. It is our opinion that we all must act with proper decorum when we beat an opponent. Just a simple "You played well" will do. Acting like a lady or gentleman at the table will increase your stature in the poker community.

In a recent magazine interview, Annie Duke talked about table demeanor in poker: "I have noticed that some of the less-experienced players ... play up to the cameras in a way that is disrespectful to others. That loss by one player might cripple his tournament dream. At one time or another, everyone will be on the losing end of a pot. Excessive celebration is so inappropriate. A player who knocks out someone should be classy and shake the opponent's hand, and then celebrate. That's how you take care of business."

FIVE BIG MISTAKES NO-LIMIT HOLD'EM TOURNAMENT PLAYERS MAKE

By Don Vines and Shane Smith

It's not the player who makes the best moves that wins no-limit hold'em tournaments—it's the player who makes the fewest mistakes who takes home the gold and the glory! Erase these five mistakes from your game and you'll chalk up the chips.

1. UNDERBETTING THE POT

An underbet is one that is very small compared to the size of the pot. When a player bets too little on the flop, his opponents are likely to call with marginal drawing hands, or to pick up a draw on the turn, sometimes with just one overcard. Underbetting is usually a signal that the bettor is primarily a limit hold'em player or is too timid to push in enough chips.

There is a time, however, when underbetting the pot might be correct. For example suppose you flop the nuts, such as an ace-high flush or the best possible straight. You might make a small bet to an attempt to lure the second and third-nut flush draws or and inferior straight draw—and sometimes even a player with one pair—into the pot. The under-bet will not work when you have a straight unless you flop the best possible straight because with a lesser straight, there always is a redraw to a higher straight. Before betting take a moment and work through the mathematics as to how much you should bet. If there is $500 in the pot and you bet $50 or $100 then you are inviting players to come after you. If you bet the size of the pot, say $500 or $750, then you take away the proper odds for your opponents with drawing hands.

2. OVERBETTING THE POT

An overbet is one that is disproportionately large compared to the size of the pot. New players sometimes make an overbet because they think that they are protecting their hand. Wrong! The usual result is that they will only be called by opponents with a better hand.

For example, suppose the blinds are $100/$200 and a player sitting up front (an early position) raises to $2,000 before the flop with pocket jacks. An opponent who has pocket kings calls his mega-raise, and the original bettor ends up losing a big pot with his lowly jacks. "Man, was I unlucky!" he mutters. Wrong! If he had made a standard raise of three to four times the big blind with his jacks, the player with the pocket kings probably would have reraised, and he could've released his hand before the flop with a minimal loss.

When you overbet the pot, beware the consequences—if you are called, you usually will find yourself with the second-best hand.

3. CALLING WITH DRAWING HANDS

In tournament poker, playing drawing hands after the flop usually means burning up your chips. If you flop a draw to a flush or straight and someone bets in front of you, my advice is to lay the hand down because you will seldom get the right price to make the draw. If you decide to bet a drawing hand, make sure to bet a large enough amount so that you have the opportunity to win the pot right then and there. Also make sure that you are drawing to the nuts. Too many players bust out of tournaments by chasing draws that are not the nuts, and by not taking the pot odds into consideration.

If you do play a drawing hand, I recommend playing it on the backside (from a late position) where you might get a free card if everyone checks the flop. The best advice is to not chase (play past the flop) when it costs to stay in the pot with drawing hands. You will last longer in the tournament, and thus allow yourself to accumulate chips with other playable hands.

4. NOT UNDERSTANDING WHEN ANOTHER PLAYER IS POT-COMMITTED

When a player raises 50 percent or more of his chips, he is pot-committed. That is, he is committed to playing the pot to the river. The player is making a statement: "I am prepared to bet all my chips on this hand." If you are considering playing the hand against the raiser, you must ask yourself, "Is my opponent pot-committed? If so, what do I need in order to call his raise?" Obviously, you will want to have a premium hand because, in most cases, after a player raises 50 percent or more of his chips before the flop, he will commit the balance of his chips on the flop.

As a rule of thumb, when you have a hand that will make you pot-committed if you raise, go ahead and raise all-in. Do not save a few chips, go for it right there. If you are going to win, you will win more. If you have a les-than-premium hand, the chances are better that your opponents will dump their hands.

For example suppose you have a pocket pair and are first to act. The blinds are $100/$200 and you have $1,200 in chips. Your normal raise would be to $700-$800, which would leave you with only $400 in chips, too few to maintain a competitive position. Since you will be pot-committed anyway, why not just move all-in instead of making your standard raise? If you get called, so be it; but in many cases, you will win the pot right then as your opponents will not want to risk doubling you up. Going all-in usually will block out marginal calling hands such as A-J, K-Q or A-10. Whereas opponents might have called a standard raise, they probably will not call an all-in move.

"What does poker break down to in the long run? Most of the money you make comes from somebody's mistakes. Good players also make mistakes, but they make fewer of them."

T.J. Cloutier, author of How to Win the Championship and member of the Poker Hall of Fame

5. CALLING BETS WITH A HAND THAT MUST IMPROVE TO WIN.

No-limit hold'em, or as we call it "big-bet poker," is a game in which hands are usually played heads-up or three-handed. If you don't think that you have the best hand, fold and save your valuable chips for a better opportunity.

Calling with second or third pair is a recipe for disaster that can cost you lots of chips. Even in rebuy tournaments where you can buy more chips when you go broke, it is still questionable whether you should get involved in a hand unless you have proper pot odds and are prepared to rebuy.

Avoid making these five critical mistakes in no-limit hold'em tournaments, and your chips will grow. Otherwise your stack will go south, and you'll be heading for the door with the four-letter word on it: Exit.

WHAT MAKES A NO-LIMIT HOLD'EM TOURNAMENT A GOOD ONE?

By Don Vines

Not all tournaments are created equal. I'm not just talking about the difference between small events and big ones. It doesn't matter whether you're playing a tournament that costs the price of a movie ticket and popcorn, or a major event that decimates a month's salary at your day job. And it's not important whether you're playing in a casino against 60 opponents or online against 600. None of these factors are important to your tournament success.

So what is?

The most important feature of a no-limit hold'em tournament is its structure. How many chips do you get to start with in relation to the size of the blinds? How long is each round of play? How much do the blinds increase at the start of each new round? The answers to these three questions determine whether a tournament is "player friendly"—and should be the main reason why you decide to play a no-limit tournament or catch a good movie instead. Let's take a closer look at each of these three elements and note how they interact with each other.

1. HOW MANY CHIPS DO YOU GET TO START WITH IN RELATION TO THE SIZE OF THE BLINDS?

The number of chips each player receives at the beginning of the tournament in relationship to the size of the blinds is very important. I've heard small buy-in tournament players say, "Wow, they give us $1,000 in starting chips!" and think they're in poker heaven. But if the starting blinds are $50/$100, they're closer to poker hell than heaven because they have only 10 times the size of the big blind to start with. You want to receive chips worth 40 or more times the big blind. For example, if the blinds start at $15/$25, you want to receive $1,000 in tournament chips at the start, enough to meet the 40 to 1 you should receive.

2. HOW LONG IS EACH ROUND OF PLAY?

The length of the rounds is the second important factor in a player-friendly tournament. The shorter the rounds, the more significant the luck factor becomes. The longer the rounds, the more your level of skill comes into play. Most $500 and higher buy-in tournament have 40 to 60 minute rounds. If the rounds are 30 minutes or less, I suggest that you do not enter the event. You need the longer rounds so that you won't feel pressured to play inferior hands such as A-7 offsuit out of position. You want to have enough time to work with your chips so that if you lose a hand, you'll still have enough ammunition to fire another round. With 45-minute rounds and 40 times the size of the big blind in starting chips, for example, you have the right amount of chips and enough time to play good tournament strategy without taking unnecessary risks to try to build your chip stack.

3. HOW MUCH DO THE BLINDS INCREASE AT THE START OF EACH NEW ROUND?

The size of the incremental increases in the blinds at the start of each new round is the third element of a good tournament. The slower the blinds increase, the more player-friendly the tournament is. In the old days of tournament poker, the blinds doubled at the start of each new round. Tex Morgan's computer program (Tex's Tears, as it is commonly called) helped tournament directors understand that they could run tournaments without doubling the blinds every round and still get the tournament over within a reasonable amount of time.

In many of today's tournaments, the size of the blinds doubles for the first three rounds, after which the blinds move up at the rate of about 50 percent per round. This structure is a little fast in the beginning, but it makes up for the fast start by slowing the increases in the blinds after the third limit. And in the late rounds, the increases slow even further, which gives players more bang for their buck the deeper they go into the event. A lot of big buy-in tournament players prefer this type of structure because, if they cannot build competitive chip stacks early in the tournament, they can get back into their usual high-stakes cash games where they make their daily bread.

No matter how fast the rounds, you want to maintain your chip stack at about 20 or more times the size of the big blind. In other words, so long as you are able to build your stack in each round or, at the lease, maintain your chip position, you're still in the chase.

OTHER ELEMENTS OF A GOOD TOURNAMENT

In our book, *How to Win No-Limit Hold'em Tournaments*, Tom McEvoy and I list several other factors that contribute to making a tournament a good investment rather than a bad bet for your bankroll. A reasonable distribution of the prize money is also important. I estimate that players make some sort of money save among themselves in 80 percent of tournaments. Since some type of money deal is made at the final table in the vast majority of poker tournaments, having the top prize no more than 36 percent is favorable. A reasonable distribution for second place might be around 19 percent, with about 9.5 percent going to the third place winner, and 6 percent awarded to the fourth-place finisher. In some of the older tournament formats, 50 percent or more went to the winner with 20 percent or less going to second place, a money distribution that was disproportionate to the total prize pool. Having the top spots closer to each other in distribution is a favorable factor.

Rebuy tournaments that don't allow a lot of rebuys, or ones that have a limited time for rebuys (such as one or two levels, or for no more than the first hour) are preferable to those that allow rebuys for three rounds or for three hours. The limited rebuy period keeps rebuys within reason and still gives players the opportunity to accumulate decent amounts of chips while swelling the prize fund. As long as the rebuys are within reason and I am still getting 50 times my accumulated buy-ins if I am fortunate enough to win, I think that I am getting a good tournament value.

Finally, floor personnel and tournament dealers are an integral part of any good tournament. I like floor persons who make fair and consistent decisions, and show the players that their patronage is appreciated. I greatly value these three qualities in tournament dealers: First, I want a dealer who is efficient and gets a lot of hands out in each round. Secondly, I like dealers who make few errors and apologize when they occasionally goof up. And I prefer dealers who are friendly yet not intrusive in their table demeanor.

One last hint: Before you plunk your buy-in onto the green felt, ask for a tournament structure sheet that lists the number of starting chips, the size of the starting blinds, the length of the rounds, and the incremental increases. If it follows the guidelines I've listed, go for the gold! If it doesn't, head for the door.

FIVE TIPS FOR WINNING NO-LIMIT HOLD'EM TOURNAMENTS

By Don Vines

How do the champions of poker win tournaments year after year? Sure, they are highly skilled players, but you can be assured that they also practice these five time-tested tactics for reaching poker's highest pinnacle.

1. PLAN YOUR ATTACK

The old business axiom, "Plan your work and work your plan" is good advice for no-limit hold'em tournament players. Decide in advance what your overall plan of attack is going to be, and then stick to it. All of today's championship events in major tournaments are multiday tournaments that require a long-term strategy. I suggest that you play solid-aggressive poker. Play only premium hands in prime position. After you establish your solid-aggressive table image, you can occasionally steal the blinds and antes. Your goal for the first day is to build your stack so that by the end of day one, you have four or more times the amount of chips that you started with. This will give you more chips than the average stack size.

You can loosen up your play during the second day by adding suited connectors to your mix of starting hands, as well as being more liberal in your raises in order to steal the blinds and antes. Projecting a solid-aggressive image will help you win pots even when you don't have a monster hand. Your goal for the second day is to increase your chip stack once again by four times the amount with which you finished day one. By the end of day two, you should be very close to the money.

On the third day you can push the risk factor a little farther by raising with any pocket pair. Identify the players at your table who are just trying to stay alive in order to make the money. You can pound these opponents into submission because they will surrender their hands unless they have monster cards. Once you've reached the money, the play loosens up considerably. Go back to playing solid-aggressive poker. You will see a lot of short stacks eliminated as they try to "double up or get up." Avoid these situations.

Once you are in the money, your goal is to increase your chip stack size to have a better chance of making it to the final table. If you have a large stack, you can pick on the short stacks who want to move up a notch. The other big stacks don't want to play against you because if they lose, they will become either a short stack or get eliminated. Be careful about confronting medium stacks—if they have a hand, they will play with you because they want to graduate to one of the big stacks. And if they win a pot from you, guess what? You become a short stack.

By the fourth day you should be at the final table or very close to it. If you are close to the final table, pound on the short stacks knowing that they will fold most hands because they're trying to squeak into the final table. Congratulations! You've made the final table. Now you want to win the tournament. Initially play solid-aggressive poker to reestablish your table image. Sit back and let the short stacks knock themselves out. Allow someone else to play "Sheriff." Once you get down to the final three where you can win the big money, you're positioned to win the tournament. Go get 'em and good luck!

2. PLAY YOUR OPPONENTS

What if the cards aren't cooperating? Oops! Now you must play the players, not just your cards. Your goal is to remain patient, as the cards will eventually come. However, if you are reading your opponents' play properly and are in late position, opportunities will come up where you can either steal the pot from the initial raiser or at least pick up the blinds. Your plan is to raise with cards such as A-x, K-9, and J-10 to just stay alive. For example, suppose you're in the cutoff seat, no one has entered the pot, and you know that the player on the button and the guy in the big blind are weak-tight players who wouldn't dare bet unless they had a premium hand. You look down to find Q-10 offsuit. Bingo! In go your chips for a raise. They fold and you pick up the antes and blinds. Every time you steal the blinds and antes, you have earned a free round of play.

3. BLUFF IN THE RIGHT SPOTS

Practice your skill at bluffing. Always know what your reasoning is behind your bluff. Do you want to win the pot right on the spot? Or are you hoping to set up a later play? As an example, you may bluff at the pot from late position when you have a hand that is not the nuts at the moment, but which has the potential to become the nuts. Suppose you have called from the cutoff seat with the A♥-5♥. The flop comes Q♥-5♠-2♥.

YOU **FLOP**

Now someone bets and wham! You bluff-raise the pot. You could win the hand right away, or if your opponent calls, you're drawing to an overcard (your A♥) and any heart to complete the nut flush. You are setting up your turn-card play with your bluff-raise on the flop. Another time to bluff is when no one has entered the pot and you are sitting on the button. The pot is "for sale," so you push in a bluff-bet to try to buy it—whether you have a legitimate hand or not. Chances are good that you'll pick up some cheap real estate.

4. BE PATIENT BEFORE YOU POUNCE

To do well in No-Limit Hold'em tournaments you must have patience, position and aggression. Patiently wait for good hands in the correct position, and then play them aggressively. Always be aware of opportunities where you can double up or significantly improve your chip position cheaply. "When you are playing to win, position is very important," Daniel Negreanu advised. "Play against shorter stacks than yours whenever possible."

5. MAKE YOUR MOVE

You've been patient, played your position strongly, and bet aggressively. Despite your best efforts, your chips have evaporated like dewdrops in the desert sun. Now what? Sometimes you just have to make a move and confidently charge full-steam ahead—with or without good cards! Never allow yourself to become so short on chips that you can be anted and blinded out of a tournament. If you have only seven times the amount of the big blind, you must move with any two high cards or with ace-anything. If you can survive the dry spell, you have a good chance of carrying out your plan—staying alive long enough to win all the marbles.

11. LETTERS TO THE POKER DOCTOR

When I first began playing poker, I had some heavy habits that dragged me down. Like a thorn in my side, these negative styles began to gouge me, leaving me **stuck** (losing) a lot of the time. I wish I'd had the sage advice of the Poker Doctor to remedy my ills. Luckily, I came across this wise physician by finally listening to P.C. Here are some of the doctor's remedies for poker maladies.

DEAR POKER DOCTOR,

I love to play poker. In fact, I love it so much that I never seem to know when to quit. Last week I played for ten hours at one session. I was ahead a lot of money after about four hours, but I stayed until I actually lost all of it back, plus some. What can I do to get the glue out of my derrière?

Outa Control in Ohio

Dear Ohio Outa,

A woman who had been in therapy for over ten years to solve her nail-biting habit consulted Dr. Wayne Dyer, famous psychologist and author of *Your Erroneous Zones*. His advice was simple: "Don't ever put your fingers in your mouth again."

One thing you can do to solve your problem is to stop playing poker. Short of such drastic measures, here are some other remedies: Set goals for yourself and stick to them at the table. For example, "I will leave at 10:00, whether I'm winning or losing." Or, "When I've won X-dollars or lost X-dollars, I will leave." Then follow Nike's advice and *"Just do it!"*

Another solution is to plan an event that you must attend at a particular hour. Or have someone call you and actually tell you to go home. One former long-hours addict invested $25 in a Timex with an alarm function. When it dinged, he darted for the door.

Winning poker players are in control of their time, money and energy *all the time*. If they play a long session, it's because they have a definite reason, such as being in a very good game in which they believe they have the maximum winning potential.

What are your reasons for playing long hours? Are you bored, using poker as a distraction from the tedium? Are you there just for fun? Or are you into a compulsive habit? During your next session, ask your poker conscience, "Why am I here right now?" If you come up with a nasty answer, such as "I'm depressed and need a lift," or "I really don't want to go home," or "I'm losing and want to win it all back tonight" (the worst of all reasons), you're in for some rocky roads on your way to Tap City.

Clean up your act before you get cleaned out at the tables. Remember, you are the one who controls your actions all the time.

The Poker Doctor

DEAR POKER DOCTOR,

I'm not sure this has anything to do with poker, but I'm desperate for an answer. It seems like I used to be a pretty good player. I was winning regularly and enjoying my lifestyle. But lately, I haven't been able to drag one pot in a hundred. Of course, I've been distracted by some personal problems that have come up all at once. Got any suggestions for me?

Perplexed in Peoria

Dear P. Peoria,

Let me give you my S.R.U. (Stop, Read, Use) formula for self-improvement. Suggestion number one: Stop playing until your personal problems are resolved. Suggestion number two: Read Bob Ciaffone's *Improve Your Poker*. Suggestion number three: Use the following guide to problem solving to work out the kinks in your life.

1. Define your problem
2. Analyze all the reasons for it
3. List 20 solutions to it
4. Select your top three ideas
5. Make a plan for one of them
6. Take action on your plan
7. Evaluate the results
8. Revise your plan if you need to
9. Take action on your revisions
10. Play poker again

Focus all your energy on solutions, not problems. Ask yourself, "What can I do *today* that would help?" Then do yourself a favor—stop sobbing and start solving.

The Poker Doctor

DEAR POKER DOCTOR,
Last night I got involved in the wildest game of Omaha high-low this side of the roller coaster at Six Flags Magic Mountain. They were playing looser than a goose with nothing but trash. I wasn't catching any cards and frankly, I was intimidated by the fast action, so I just stayed out of most of it (would've won a coupla times if I'd been in it.) How do I handle games like this?

Timid in Texas

Dear Texas Tim,

One fundamental poker skill is adjusting your play to the style of the game. Although you are correct in playing disciplined poker in a very loose game, if you're playing tight-as-a-vacuum-sealed frozen food dinner in a loose game, you'll miss some good opportunities for profit. In high action games, you may have to enter more pots than you ordinarily would to get the best of it. But if it's so loose that your emotional state can't handle it, leave the table.

A game sometimes has "seasons." For a while, it might be hotter than August in Las Vegas, then it might cool off, usually when the maniacs get tapped out and decide to wait for better starting hands. Also, after a megapot betting round, there is often a letdown of emotions and the next hand will be a Clark Kent yawner. You can either ride out the wild wave and wait for the evening tide, or you can come in with somewhat lower standards and try to reap part of the harvest during the loose season.

Your strategy partly depends on how your cards are running. When you're losing, you need to play tighter (often, against your natural instincts). But when you're winning, you can take advantage of your stronger table image and play faster than you usually would.

Here's another idea for you, Texas Timid: How about trying on the hat of Bold Bob for a session or two? If it fits, fine. If it doesn't, fold. Of course, you could take both hats with you to the game, right?

The Poker Doctor

DEAR POKER DOCTOR,

I'm a "chronic"—a chronic caller, a dyed-in-the-wool loose goose with zilch discipline. I love the action. I hate the boredom of waiting around for premium hands. And I'm a loser. Help!

Loose in Louisville

Dear Loose Louie,

Help is on its way. The bottom line of playing profitable poker is the big "D"—discipline. You can *know* all the right stuff, but until you do the right stuff, you'll get it stuffed up your nose every time you play. So here are some ideas for you:

1. For 30 minutes (make it 15 minutes if that's too much of a challenge for you in the beginning), play only *wheel* hands in Omaha high-low (an ace with three cards lower than a 7). Then for the next 30 minutes (15?), enter pots with only high hands (four cards higher than an 8). Or in Texas hold'em, play *only* the starting hands by position listed in Lou Krieger's *Hold'em Excellence*. Or religiously follow the step-by-step missions in Caro's *11 Days to 7-Stud Success* or his *12 Days to Hold'em Success*.

   In other words, play two games at once—one with yourself and one with the other players. These mental maneuvers are designed to help you develop the big "D" for yourself.

2. Make a game plan one hour before you begin to play. Affirm to yourself that you will follow it, *no matter what*. Write it on a business card and place it between you and your chips so that you can read it before every hand you play.

continued

continued

3. Every 30 minutes, write down the amount of money that
you have in front of you. Rate your play on a scale of 1-
10: 1 meaning loose-as-a-goose, 10 standing for tight as a
rusty cap on a can of Coors. Record all your rebuys. At
the end of the session, analyze your chart. When did you
make the most money? Lose the most? Stay even? Under
what playing conditions did you do the best?

These mental games will keep you busy while you're waiting for a
hand, and will make you *think* about everything you do at the table.
You can also schedule breaks at the one-hour marks, or go to the
john (your private think tank) and review your notes. You can even
pretend that you are your favorite Poker Hero and ask yourself, "If I
were (name your flame), what would I do now?" Then do it!

Some of the enemies of self discipline—I prefer *control*—are boredom, a need for excitement, fatigue, hunger, frustration, anger, de-
pression, mania (the feeling that you cannot lose), revenge, showing
off, and laziness (not doing what you know you need to do to win).
Pinpoint your biggest enemy and look him square in the face—then
when you begin to feel his ominous presence, leave the table to mentally consult your Poker Hero (or my favorite advisor, P.C.)

Healthy human beings move *toward* pleasure and *away from* pain.
Avoidance-of-pain is actually stronger for most people than seeking
pleasure. So, the more you can move away from the pain that a lack
of self control brings you, the closer you will move toward the pleasure that playing profitable poker can give you.

Thanks for an honest letter. Now dig in so that you can dig out!

The Poker Doctor

12. CONCLUDING REMARKS

So now you've read the book and you've played a lot of low-limit poker—and hopefully, you've won a lot of money. Now what? Enjoy, that's what! Enjoy yourself at the tables by looking at each session as an adventure into the domain of profit and pleasure.

Think of yourself as a knight whose armor is impenetrable and whose arsenal of weapons is limitless. You are going to slay the dragons of poker. But beware The Shadow, that dark side of your poker psyche who tempts you to fight too many battles and refuses to lay down your arms in the face of a mightier combatant.

You can defang The Shadow with knowledge, skill, discipline and a positive mental attitude. Before every session, recite your Poker Mission Statement to him. It might sound something like this:

My mission as a poker player is to gain both profit and pleasure by playing the right hands right. I will wait and watch so that I can win.

You can bring The Shadow to his knees by reciting your poker affirmations to him every time he rears his ugly face and tries to disempower you. Each one of your mental reminders can destroy one of his shady sides and shore up your weaknesses. Some of my favorites are:

- Play tight and right.
- Fold when you know you're beat.
- Wait ... watch ... win
- Leave when you're not playing your best game
- Stay in control

When you can control your behavior at the poker table, when you know enough strategies to give you an edge over your opponents, and when you maintain a positive attitude during every minute of your playing time, you will have the sword to slay your personal poker dragons.

The best of luck to you!

You have to pay your dues. Poker is like going to school. Some quit before finishing high school, some stop after high school or college, and others get their master's degree. But the best never quit learning.
—*Johnny Chan*

The only bad luck for a gambler is bad health. The rest is just temporary aggravation.
—*Benny Binion*

Most people make their own luck, or they create their own misfortune.
—*Tex Sheahan*

13. GLOSSARY

Act To choose a betting option. "When it's your turn to *act*, you can do one of four things—check, fold, call or raise."

Add on Buy more chips at the end of the rebuy period in rebuy tournaments, usually after the first three rounds of play. "I had so many chips when the rebuy period was over, I didn't need to make the *add on*."

Any ace In Texas hold'em, an ace in the hole with a bad second card that doesn't help the ace. "I knew I shouldn't have called with my A-8, and sure enough, I lost a big pot to an A-Q. No more *any-ace* hands for me!"

Backdoor a flush/ straight Make a hand that you were not originally drawing to by catching favorable cards on later streets. "I'd been betting the nut low draw, but when a third diamond came on the board, I *backdoored* a flush."

Backup A card that gives you an extra out. "You always want an extra low card in Omaha high-low to *back up* your ace-deuce."

Bad beat When a very good "made" hand gets beaten on a later street, often by a hand of lesser value. "I raised before the flop with pocket aces and flopped trips, but suffered a *bad beat* when Henry, who called with a 10-9 suited, made a flush on the river."

Behind Getting to act after other players have acted. "So long as you're sitting *behind* your opponents, you have the advantage of position."

Big ace An ace with a big kicker (A-K or A-Q). "When the flop came A-6-2 in hold'em, I played my *big ace* strong."

Big blind The larger of two mandatory bets equal to the maximum flop bet that you must post before the flop in Omaha and hold'em games when you are sitting two seats to the left of the dealer button. "Since I was the *big blind* and already had a full bet in the pot, I decided to call Roy's pre-flop raise."

Big flop The flop comes with cards that greatly improve the strength of your hand. "I caught a *big flop* that gave me the nut flush, a wheel, and a set."

Big slick An A-K hand, suited or unsuited (one of the strongest starting hands in hold'em). "When I looked down to see that I'd been dealt *big slick* suited in spades, I raised the pot three times the size of the big blind."

Blind A forced bet that players must make to get the action started in hold'em games. The small blind must post one-half the opening bet; the big blind must place a full bet before the deal begins. "When I'm in the small *blind*, I'll gladly just fold and give up my *blind* money if I don't have premium cards."

Board The cards that are dealt face-up in the middle of the table in Omaha and hold'em to make your best possible five-card hand. "It's been hard to remember that I have to use three *board* cards in Omaha high-low."

Boss hand A hand that is the best possible high hand. "In Omaha high-low, when you have the *boss* high *hand*, you should bet it as aggressively as possible, especially if you think two low hands are out there."

Bully   Playing aggressively. "When I have a big stack in a tournament, I like being able to *bully* the entire table."

Bunching factor   A phrase coined by Tom McEvoy to describe a situation when early and middle position players fold before the flop, presuming that big cards are "bunched" behind you, often in the blind hands. "I was on the button and no one had entered the pot, but I decided not to bluff with my weak cards because I thought that the good cards might be *bunched* behind me in the blinds."

Call   Match the size of the required bet. "I decided to just *call* rather than raise with my nut flush draw."

Cap   The limit to the number of raises the house rules allow. "I couldn't play my 7-6 suited in the small blind because Sandra had *capped* the pot before it got to me."

Cash game   A poker game played for money in which you can buy more chips any time you want to, and you can begin or stop playing at any time. "I prefer playing *cash games* because I can always reach into my pocket and replenish my chip supply when I run low, and I can leave whenever I've won enough or lost too much."

Change gears   Adjust your style of play from fast to slow, from loose to tight, from raising to calling, and so on. "When the cards quit coming his way, Will didn't *change gears*; instead, he kept on playing fast and lost his whole bankroll."

Check   `Decline to wager when you are the first player to act and no bets are due. "After the flop in hold'em games, you can pass play on to the next player and still remain active by simply *checking*."

Cold call Call a raise without having put an initial bet into the pot. "Brunson raised, Hellmuth reraised, and I *cold called*."

Come over the top Raise or reraise. "I raised it $2,000 and Sexton *came over the top* of me with $7,000."

Commit fully Put in as many chips as necessary to play your hand to the river, even if they are your last chips. "If I think the odds are in my favor, I will *fully commit*."

Community cards (the Board) In hold'em games, the cards that the dealer places face up in the center of the table for you to combine with your hole cards in order to make your best possible hand. "The board came with *community cards* that didn't match my hole cards, so I folded."

Connectors Cards that are adjacent to each other in rank, such as 7-6 or K-Q. "T.J. suggests playing middle *connectors* such as 8-7 in late position only in tournament hold'em games."

Counterfeited In Omaha high-low, when your nut low hand gets demoted by cards on the board that duplicate your hole cards. "You should always have a third low card to protect you're A-2 against getting *counterfeited*."

Cutoff seat The late-position seat at the poker table that is one place to the right of the button. "I sometimes like to try bluffing from the cutoff *seat*, especially if I think the button will fold."

Dangler A fourth card that doesn't fit in with your other three cards in Omaha games. "K-Q-J-6, three high cards with a *dangler*—who wants to play that kind of hand? That dangler can put you in a world of misery."

Decision hand A hand that requires you to make a value judgment. "The great hands and the trash hands play themselves. It is how all of the marginal, in-between hands—the *decision* hands—are played that separate winners from losers."

Family pot A pot that almost every player has entered. "I loved playing that loose-passive Omaha game last night because on almost every deal, we had a *family pot.*"

Flat call You call a bet without raising. "When he bet in front of me, I just *flat called* to keep the players behind me from folding."

Flop The first three community cards the dealer places in the center of the table after the first round of betting in a hold'em or Omaha game. "I threw away my high cards on the low-card *flop* because Shane preaches 'fit or fold' in Omaha high-low."

Flop to it The flop enhances the value of your hand. "If you don't *flop to it*, you can get away from the hand."

Fold Get rid of your cards and become inactive in the hand. "*Folding* indicates that you do not wish to match the bets required and opt out of play."

Freezeout tournament A poker tournament in which you cannot buy more chips when you go broke. "Jim told me he prefers playing *freezeout*, no-rebuy tournaments because when players go broke, they're out of action and the field he has to beat gets that much smaller."

Full-kill A poker game in which the stakes double under special circumstances dictated by the house rules. "Jennifer likes to play *full-kill* games in which the stakes double on the next hand after someone wins two pots in a row."

**Get away
from it**   Fold, what usually appears to be a premium hand until an unfavorable flop negates its potential. "If you don't flop to the low, *get away from* it."

Get full value   Bet, raise and reraise to manipulate the size of the pot so that you will win the maximum number of chips if you win the hand. "By raising on every round, I was able to get *full value* when my hand held up at the river."

Get there   To make your hand. "When you *get there*, you might be able to start maximizing your bets."

Half-kill   A poker game in which the stakes increase by 50 percent under special circumstances dictated by the house rules. "After I had won two pots in a row in my $4/$8 Omaha high-low game with a *half-kill*, I had to put in a forced blind bet of $6 on the next hand when the limits rose to $6/$12."

Hole cards   The cards you are dealt facedown in hold'em games; also called your "hand." "I had aces in the *hole* and raised the pot."

Jammed pot   The pot is raised the maximum number of times, and may also be multiway. "You should pass with a weak hand if the pot has been *jammed* before it gets to you."

Key card   The one card that will make your hand a winner. "I knew that I needed to catch a deuce, the *key card* to my wheel draw."

Kicker   The second-highest card you have in the hole in Texas hold'em. "With my K-10 in the hole, I realized that if I hit a king on the flop, I would have a weak *kicker*."

Lay down   Fold. "In no-limit hold'em, you can raise enough chips to blow everybody away and sometimes even get the raiser to *lay down* his hand."

Limit hold'em A hold'em game in which the blinds and bets are limited to a prescribed amount of money. "Whenever I go into my favorite cardroom, the waiting list for *limit hold'em* is about five times longer than the list for no-limit hold'em."

Limp Enter the pot by just calling rather than raising. "In Omaha high-low you might want to *limp in* from up front with a premium low hand such as A-2-4-5."

Limper(s) Players who enter the pot for the minimum bet. "With three *limpers* in the pot, I thought that my pair of kings probably was the best hand."

Live cards Cards that you need to improve your hand and which probably are still available to you. "When three players who I knew to be big-pair players entered the pot in front of me, I thought my middle connectors might still be *live* so I decided to play the hand."

Low wrap The cards in your hand will make a low straight if one other connecting low card hits the board. "When the 3-6-7 hit the board, I had the *low wrap* with my A-2-4-8."

Make a move Try to bluff. "When the board paired sixes, Shane *made a move* at the pot. I thought he was bluffing but I had nothing to call with."

Multiway Three or more players in a pot. "In low-limit Omaha high-low games, most pots are played *multiway*, sometimes with as many as seven players."

No-limit hold'em A hold'em game in which players can bet as much money as they have in front of them at any time, in contrast to limit hold'em in which the bets are limited to prescribed amounts. "Be prepared to go broke fast in a *no-limit hold'em* game if you go all in and lose the hand."

Nut draw   You have a draw to the best possible hand. "When two clubs come on the board and you have the A-4 of clubs, you have the *nut* flush *draw*."

Nuts   The best hand possible at the moment. "Remember that you can flop the *nuts* and lose it on the turn, especially in Omaha high-low."

Offsuit   Cards that are not the same suit. "I couldn't believe it when Daniel turned over a 9-7 *offsuit* and won the pot by making a straight against my two pair."

Out (an)   A card that completes or improves your hand. "Always try to have an extra *out*, a third low card to go with your ace, when you're drawing for the low end."

Overpair   You have a pair in your hand that is higher than the highest card showing on the board. "I flopped an *overpair*, but folded against the action in front of me."

Pay off   You call an opponent's bet at the river even though you think that he might have the best hand. "I decided to *pay him off* when the board paired at the river and he bet—I didn't think that he'd made trips."

Play back   Responding to an opponent's bet by either raising or reraising. "If a tight opponent *plays back* at you, you know he probably has the nuts."

Play fast   Bet aggressively. "Many players *play fast* in the early rounds of rebuy tournaments to try to build their stacks."

Play slow   Bet conservatively, checking or calling, as opposed to betting and raising. "When you make the nut straight on the flop and there's a chance that the flush draw is out there, why not play your hand *slow* to start with?"

Play with Staying in the hand by betting, calling, raising or re-raising. "You should realize that in Omaha high-low, you're going to *get played with* most of the time because in a limit game there usually are a lot of players in every pot."

Position Where you are sitting at the poker table in relation to the button. "When I'm sitting in late *position*, one or two seats to the right of the dealer, I can play more hands."

Pot (the) The money that players have wagered and which sits in the middle of the table. "The *pot* is what I'm trying to win on each deal."

Put them on (a hand) You assign a value to your opponent's hand. "Using my instincts and the way he had played the hand, I *put Stanley on* the nut low."

Rag (or blank) A board card that doesn't help you and appears not to have helped anyone else, either. "The flop came with A-2-3 and then a *rag* 9 hit on the turn."

Rag off The river card doesn't help you. "Then it *ragged off* on the end and he lost all his money."

Rainbow flop The flop cards are three different suits. "I liked my straight draw when the flop came *rainbow* and nobody could have a flush draw against me."

Raise Increase the bet size by making a bigger bet than one currently in action. "After six players had entered the pot for the minimum $8-bet, Roy pushed in $16 and proudly announced '*Raise!*'"

Rake The amount of money the host casino takes from each pot to cover its expenses and profits. "If I don't like the amount of the *rake* the house takes, I'll play at a different casino that is more reasonable."

Read the board Understand the value of your hand in relation to the cards on the board. "If you *read the board* correctly, you often can tell by the action who has a high hand and who has a low hand."

Rebuy tournament A poker tournament in which you can buy more chips when you go broke or when your stack shrinks below a predetermined minimum. "Most casinos allow *rebuys* during only the first three rounds of the tournament, but I have played events in which you could only make one rebuy."

Reraise Raise after someone has already raised in front of you. "When Fast Eddie raised from the cutoff seat, I immediately *reraised* on the button to shut out the blinds and get heads-up with my nemesis."

River The fifth and final community card that the dealer turns up in hold'em games. Also called fifth street. "When the board paired on the *river*, I made a full house and raked in a big pot."

Rock A very conservative player who always waits for premium cards before he plays a hand. "Smith was playing like a *rock* so when she bet in front of me, I knew she had me beat."

Run over Playing aggressively in an attempt to control the other players. "If they're not trying to stop you from being a bully, then keep *running over them* until they do."

Runner-runner Catch cards on the turn and river that make your hand a winner. "He had a suited K-J against my A-K, but caught *runner-runner* to make a flush and break me!"

Safe card   A card dealt on the board that does not appear to help your opponents. "I made the nut heart flush on the flop, so I was hoping for *safe* cards on the turn and river, such as a spade that didn't pair the board or even another heart."

Satellite   A preliminary tournament with a comparatively low buy-in that awards seats into a bigger event with a higher buy-in. "When Tom won the $10,000 buy-in World Series of Poker, he entered the tournament by winning his seat in a $1,000 buy-in *satellite*."

Scoop the pot   You win both the high and low ends of a pot in a split-pot game. "The whole idea of Omaha high-low is to play hands that you can *scoop the pot* with."

Scooper   A hand that wins the whole pot. "When a third low card failed to come at the river, I had a *scooper* with my high hand."

Second nut   A hand that is second to the best possible hand at the moment. "Bob was surprised when his ace-high, *second-nut* flush lost to Erick's straight flush on the river."

Sheriff   A slang word for a player who calls too many hands, primarily in limit poker, in the hope of catching his opponents bluffing. "If you keep on playing *sheriff* and trying to keep players honest, you're liable to go broke, Mary warned Jay when he called her on the river with only a low pair."

Showdown   When the cards are turned over on the river to determine the winner. "If everyone checks to you at the river and you couldn't win in a *showdown*, why bet if you know that you will get called?"

Side game   A poker game that is played for cash while a nearby tournament is in progress. "Bob attends all the big pot-limit tournaments in the South looking for *side games* he can beat for big bucks."

Slowplay   You intentionally do not bet a strong hand because you are hoping to trap your opponents. "You usually can't give free cards in Omaha—you don't *slowplay*, you play very straightforwardly. If you have it, bet it."

Smooth call   Call a bet without raising. "If someone bets into you, you might *smooth call* when you have an extra out to a better hand."

Stand a raise   Call a raise. "I recently *stood a raise* in a cash game with 9-9 on the button, a hand I couldn't have called with from early position."

Structure   The design of a tournament, including whether it is a freezeout or a rebuy event. "The *structure* of the main event at the World Series of Poker is excellent because you start with $10,000 in chips and the opening rounds last for an hour."

Suited   Two or more cards of the same suit: spades, hearts, diamonds, clubs. "If Barbara's connecting hole cards aren't *suited*, she won't play the hand."

Take off a card   Call a bet so that an additional card can be seen. "I decided to *take off a card* and see what the turn would bring."

Third nut   The third best hand possible at the moment. "I really goofed up when I called a bet on the river in my Omaha high-low game with the *third nut* low, an A-4."

Tournament   A poker contest in which players are eliminated when they run out of chips, and the last player remaining is declared the winner. "*Tournaments* are getting tougher to win these days because the fields are so much bigger and the players are so much stronger than they were back in the '80s."

Turn   The fourth community card in hold'em and Omaha that the dealer places in the center next to the three flop cards—also called fourth street. "My nut-low draw got counterfeited on the *turn* when the dealer turned up an ace."

Under the gun The first player to act—the first seat to the left of the big blind. "T.J. suggests that you raise with pocket aces, even if you're *under the gun.*"

Underbet When you make a bet in no-limit hold'em that is considerably smaller than the typical bet made for the situation. "You don't make a small bet to try to pick up a big pot. The *underbet* is a tip-off that you have a big hand."

Underpair You hold a pair that is lower than the highest card showing on the board. "Why would you ever want to call with an *underpair?*"

Unsuited Cards of different suits. "When I made my straight on the turn, I was glad to see that the board was *unsuited* so that no flush was possible."

Up front A seat position at the poker table that is one or two seats to the left of the big blind. "When you're sitting *up front* in a hold'em game, Caro suggests that you don't enter pots with anything less than aces, kings, or A-K."

Value bet A bet you make to increase the size of the pot, especially when you have a strong draw with multiple outs to win the pot. "When I made top pair on the turn with a draw to the nut flush, I *value bet* my hand so as to win a bigger pot if my cards held up on the river." (See Cardoza's *Poker Talk* for an excellent explanation of this term.)

Wake up with a hand You are dealt a strong hand. "Just because a player is a maniac doesn't mean that he can't *wake up with a hand.* Over the long haul, everybody gets the same number of good hands and bad hands."

Wheel A-2-3-4-5, the best low hand you can make in Omaha high-low poker. "When I made a *wheel* on the river, I also made a flush and scooped the pot with the nut low and the nut high."

Where you're at You understand the value of your hand in relation to the other players' hands. "Your opponent may not know for sure *where you're at* in the hand when you have played it in a deceptive way."

Wraparound (Wrap) The connectors in your hand wrap perfectly around the flop cards, giving you multiple ways to make a straight. "Suppose the flop comes 10-7-2 and you have J-9-8-6 in your hand. That's a complete *wrap*—you can catch a card on either end or in the middle and make your hand."

14. SUGGESTED POKER PRODUCTS

World Class Poker, Masque's software program for improving your game. Masque enlisted T.J. Cloutier, renowned author, multititled poker champion, and master teacher to give you video tips on each of the games on this training program. You can select limit hold'em, no-limit hold'em, or pot-limit hold'em cash games or tournaments to play. When a key hand comes up, T.J. pops up with a video recommendation about how to play your cards. You also can play five-card draw, seven-card stud, and Omaha in this action-packed computer poker tutorial. Go to www.masque.com for full information on this and other Masque gaming products.

Turbo Texas Hold'em, one of Wilson Software's many software programs, is designed to help you learn and polish your game before you set foot in a live or online casino environment. Wilson has continually improved his products through the years, expanding their artificial intelligence core to include observing and adjusting to your playing style and that of your opponents. In other words, it's hard to run over your foes on any of Wilson's Turbo poker programs, especially in tournament mode.

Poker Insight, a four-volume set of DVDs produced by Poker Entertainment LLC. Volume One—Hold'em Basics—features T.J. Cloutier, Greg Raymer, Men Nguyen, Barry Greenstein, Ted Forrest, James Worth, Tom Franklin, and Warren Karp giving you their best advice on how to win at low-limit no-limit hold'em and limit hold'em. Go to www. pokerinsight.com for further information on all four DVDs.

Beat Texas Hold'em, a pocket-book size book that Tom McEvoy and I wrote for rank beginners at hold'em. Covers limit and no-limit hold'em Internet games, cash games and tournaments. If you're a total neophyte to hold'em, this is the book for you. Probably the most value for the fewest bucks ($6.95) in the current poker market, you'll find it listed in the Cardoza Publishing pages in the back of this book.

Poker Talk (Learn How to Talk Poker Like a Pro!) by Avery Cardoza is the best poker dictionary on the market. Cardoza has been in the gaming books business for more than two decades and really knows his stuff when it comes to poker, his game of choice for recreation. I keep this dictionary on my desk and referred to it often while writing the glossary for this book. Visit www.cardozapub.com for complete information.

Championship Hold'em (How to Win Hold'em Cash Games & Tournaments) by Tom McEvoy and T.J. Cloutier is a big book (380 pages) devoted to teaching you how to play limit hold'em, the game of choice of millions of people across the globe. The authors, who have collaborated on several other important poker books, wrote this one in a unique conversational style that is both educational and entertaining. Published by Cardoza Publishing.

Championship Omaha (Omaha high-low, Omaha high and pot-limit Omaha) by Cloutier and McEvoy could become your bible on how to win at Omaha high-low. Yes, it's that good! Of course you won't find many high Omaha or pot-limit Omaha cash games these days because they're played primarily in tournament format. But don't let that deter you from reading this book—its emphasis is on Omaha high-low, with plenty of demonstration hands and tournament tips designed to turn you into a winning player. Another book in the "Championship Series" published by Cardoza Publishing.

Omaha High-Low (Winning Strategies for all 5,278 Omaha High-Low Hands) by Bill Boston is a must-have book for serious players. No matter how low or how high the stakes you play, the odds for particular types of poker hands remain the same. Boston not only gives you the odds of winning the high, the low, or scooping the pot with every conceivable Omaha high-low hand, he tells you how to win more often by using the odds to your advantage. I was fortunate in working with Boston on a few of his strategy tips, and can vouch for the precision and strength of his recommended plays. Cardoza Publishing.

Poker Tournament Tips from the Pros (How to Win Low-Limit Poker Tournaments) by Shane Smith. I first wrote this book in 1992 and updated it for today's structures and poker environment. Its value for beginning tournament players is in its simple explanation of elementary tournament principles. I clearly explain the fundamental concepts of tournament poker that so many pro players have buried in the back of their minds and take for granted that everybody knows. In the early days of poker, I self-published this book but later turned it over to the world's largest publisher of poker books, Cardoza Publishing.

How to Win No-Limit Hold'em Tournaments is a super book for beginning to intermediate no-limit hold'em players who want to dip their toes into the swift waters of no-limit tournaments. Written by tournament experts Don Vines and Tom McEvoy, this is my favorite book for newcomers to no-limit hold'em. Vines was legendary around Las Vegas for winning low-limit to mid-limit no-limit hold'em events, as well as being an expert limit hold'em and Omaha high-low player with enviable tournament results. McEvoy won the World Championship of Poker in 1983, and has followed up by winning three other World Series of Poker bracelets, as well as numerous high-limit tournaments during his 30-year poker career. The chemistry between the two authors comes through in their expert, down-to-earth advice. Another fine book from my favorite publisher, Cardoza Publishing.

GREAT CARDOZA POKER BOOKS
ADD THESE TO YOUR LIBRARY - ORDER NOW!

HOW TO WIN AT OMAHA HIGH-LOW POKER by *Mike Cappelletti*. Clearly written strategies and powerful advice shows the essential winning strategies for beating Omaha high-low poker! This money-making guide includes more than sixty hard-hitting sections on Omaha. Players learn the rules of play, best starting hands, strategies for the flop, turn, and river, how to read the board for both high and low, dangerous draws, and how to beat low-limit tournaments. Includes odds charts, glossary and low-limit tips. 304 pgs, $19.95.

OMAHA HIGH-LOW: How to Win at the Lower Limits by *Shane Smith*. New edition teaches low-limit players the essential winning strategies necesary for beating Omaha high-low. You'll learn the best starting hands, how to play the flop, turn, and river, how to read the board for both high and low, dangerous draws, and how to win low-limit tournaments. Smith shows the differences between Omaha high-low and hold'em strategies. Includes odds charts, glossary, low-limit tips, and strategic ideas. 176 pages, $12.95.

THE BIG BOOK OF POKER by *Ken Warren*. This easy-to-read and oversized guide teaches you everything you need to know to win money at home poker, in cardrooms, casinos, and on the tournament circuit. Readers will learn how to bet, raise, and checkraise, bluff, semi-bluff, and how to take advantage of position and pot odds. Great sections on hold'em (plus stud games, Omaha, draw games, and many more) and playing and winning poker on the internet. Packed with charts, diagrams, sidebars, and detailed, easy-to-read examples by best-selling poker expert Ken Warren, this wonderfully formatted book is one stop shopping for players ready to take on any form of poker for real money. Want to be a big player? Buy the Big Book of Poker! 320 oversized pages, $19.95.

WINNER'S GUIDE TO TEXAS HOLD' EM POKER by *Ken Warren*. You'll learn how to play every hand from every position with every type of flop. Learn the 14 categories of starting hands, the 10 most common hold'em tells, how to evaluate a game for profit, the value of deception, the art of bluffing, eight secrets to winning, starting hand categories, position, and more! Includes detailed analysis of the top 40 hands and the most complete chapter on hold'em odds in print. Over 400,000 copies sold! 224 pages, $14.95.

KEN WARREN TEACHES TEXAS HOLD 'EM by *Ken Warren*. This is a step-by-step comprehensive manual for making money at hold'em poker. 42 powerful chapters teach you one lesson at a time. Great practical advice and concepts with examples from actual games and how to apply them to your own play. Lessons include: Starting Cards, Playing Position, Raising, Check-raising, Tells, Game/Seat Selection, Dominated Hands, Odds, and much more. This book is already a huge fan favorite and best-seller! 416 pages, $26.95.

WINNER'S GUIDE TO OMAHA POKER by *Ken Warren*. Concise and easy-to-understand, Warren shows beginning and intermediate Omaha players how to win from the first time they play. You'll learn the rules, betting and blind structure, why you should play Omaha, the advantages of Omaha over Texas hold'em, glossary, reading the board, basic strategies, Omaha high, Omaha hi-low split 8/better, how to play draws and made hands, evaluation of starting hands, counting outs, computing pot odds, the unique characteristics of split-pot games, the best and worst Omaha hands, how to play before the flop, how to play on the flop, how to play on the turn and river, and much more. 224 pages, $19.95

CHAMPIONSHIP TOURNAMENT POKER by *Tom McEvoy*. Enthusiastically endorsed by more than five world champions, this is a *must* for every player's library. McEvoy lets you in on the secrets he has used to win millions of dollars in tournaments and the insights he has learned competing against the best players in the world. Packed solid with winning strategies for 11 games with extensive discussions of 7-card stud, limit hold'em, pot and no-limit hold'em, Omaha high-low, re-buy, half-half tournaments, satellites, and includes strategies for each stage of tournaments. 416 pages, $29.95.

GREAT CARDOZA POKER BOOKS
ADD THESE TO YOUR LIBRARY - ORDER NOW!

CRASH COURSE IN BEATING TEXAS HOLD'EM *by Avery Cardoza*. Perfect for beginning and somewhat experienced players who want to jump right in on the action and play cash games, local tournaments, online poker, and the big televised tournaments where millions of dollars can be made. Both limit and no-limit hold'em games are covered along with the essential strategies needed to play profitably on the preflop, flop, turn, and river. The good news is that you don't need to memorize hands or be burdened by math to be a winner—just play by the no-nonsense basic principles outlined here. 208 pages, $14.95

INTERNET HOLD'EM POKER *by Avery Cardoza*. Learn how to get started in the exciting world of online poker. The book concentrates on Internet no-limit hold'em, but also covers limit and pot-limit hold'em, five- and seven-card stud, and Omaha. You'll learn everything from how to play and bet safely online to playing multiple tables, using early action buttons, and finding easy opponents. Cardoza gives you the largest collection of online-specific strategies in print—more than 6,500 words dedicated to 25 unique strategies! You'll also learn how to get sign-up bonuses worth hundreds of dollars! 176 pages, $9.95

HOW TO PLAY WINNING POKER *by Avery Cardoza*. New and completely updated, this classic has sold more than 250,000 copies. Includes major new coverage on playing and winning tournaments, online poker, limit and no-limit hold'em, Omaha games, seven-card stud, and draw poker (including triple draw). Includes 21 essential winning concepts of poker, 15 concepts of bluffing, how to use psychology and body language to get an extra edge, plus information on playing online poker. 256 pages, $14.95.

POKER TALK: Learn How to Talk Poker Like a Pro *by Avery Cardoza*. This fascinating and fabulous collection of colorful poker words, phrases, and poker-speak features more than 2,000 definitions. No longer is it enough to know how to walk the walk in poker, you need to know how to talk the talk! Learn what it means to go all in on a rainbow flop with pocket rockets and get it cracked by cowboys, put a bad beat on a calling station, and go over the top of a producer fishing with a gutshot to win a big dime. You'll soon have those railbirds wondering what *you* are talking about. 304 pages, $9.95.

OMAHA HIGH-LOW: Play to Win with the Odds *by Bill Boston*. Selecting the right hands to play is the most important decision to make in Omaha. This is the *only* book that shows you the chances that every one of the 5,278 Omaha high-low hands has of winning the high end of the pot, the low end of it, and how often it is expected to scoop all the chips. You get all the vital tools needed to make critical preflop decisions based on the results of more than 500 million computerized hand simulations. You'll learn the 100 most profitable starting cards, trap hands to avoid, 49 worst hands, 30 ace-less hands you can play for profit, and the three bandit cards you must know to avoid losing hands. 248 pages, $19.95.

POKER TOURNAMENT TIPS FROM THE PROS *by Shane Smith*. Essential advice from poker theorists, authors, and tournament winners on the best strategies for winning the big prizes at low-limit rebuy tournaments. Learn the best strategies for each of the four stages of play—opening, middle, late and final—how to avoid 26 potential traps, advice on rebuys, aggressive play, clock-watching, inside moves, top 20 tips for winning tournaments, and more. Advice from McEvoy, Caro, Malmuth, Ciaffone, others. 160 pages, $14.95.

NO-LIMIT TEXAS HOLD 'EM: The New Player's Guide to Winning Poker's Biggest Game *by Brad Daugherty & Tom McEvoy*. For experienced limit players who want to play no-limit or rookies who has never played before, two world champions show readers how to evaluate the strength of a hand, determine the amount to bet, understand opponents' play, plus how to bluff and when to do it. Seventy-four game scenarios, unique betting charts for tournament play, and sections on essential principles and strategies show you how to get to the winners circle. Special section on beating online tournaments. 288 pages, $24.95.

GREAT CARDOZA POKER BOOKS
ADD THESE TO YOUR LIBRARY - ORDER NOW!

HOLD'EM WISDOM FOR ALL PLAYERS *By Daniel Negreanu.* Superstar poker player Daniel Negreanu provides 50 easy-to-read and right-to-the-point hold'em strategy nuggets that will immediately make you a better player at cash games and tournaments. His wit and wisdom makes for great reading; even better, it makes for killer winning advice. Conversational, straightforward, and educational, this book covers topics as diverse as the top 10 rookie mistakes to bullying bullies and exploiting your table image. 176 pages, $14.95.

MILLION DOLLAR HOLD'EM: Winning Big in Limit Cash Games *by Johnny Chan and Mark Karowe.* Learn how to win money consistently at limit hold'em, poker's most popular cash game, from one of poker's living legends. You'll get a rare opportunity to get into the mind of the man who has won ten World Series of Poker titles—tied for the most ever with Doyle Brunson—as Johnny picks out illustrative hands and shows how he thinks his way through the betting and the bluffing. No book so thoroughly details the thought process of how a hand is played, the alternative ways it could have been played, and the best way to win session after session. *Essential* reading for cash players. 400 pages, $29.95.

THE POKER TOURNAMENT FORMULA *by Arnold Snyder.* Start making money now in fast no-limit hold'em tournaments with these radical and never-before-published concepts and secrets for beating tournaments. You'll learn why cards don't matter as much as the dynamics of a tournament—your position, the size of your chip stack, who your opponents are, and above all, the structure. Poker tournaments offer one of the richest opportunities to come along in decades. Every so often, a book comes along that changes the way players attack a game and provides them with a big advantage over opponents. Gambling legend Arnold Snyder has written such a book. 368 pages, $19.95.

HOW TO BEAT SIT-AND-GO POKER TOURNAMENTS *by Neil Timothy.* There is a lot of dead money up for grabs in the lower limit sit-and-gos and Neil Timothy shows you how to go and get it. The author, a professional player, shows you how to reach the last six places of lower limit sit-and-go tournaments four out of five times and then how to get in the money 25-35 percent of the time using his powerful, proven strategies. This book can turn a losing sit-and-go player into a winner, and a winner into a bigger winner. Also effective for the early and middle stages of one-table satellites.184 pages, $14.95.

HOW TO BEAT LOW-LIMIT POKER *by Shane Smith and Tom McEvoy.* If you're a low-limit player frustrated by poor results or books written by high-stakes players for big buy-in games, this is exactly the book you need! You'll learn how to win big money at the little games—$1/$2, $2/$4, $4/$8, $5/$10—typically found in casinos, cardrooms and played in home poker games. After one reading, you'll lose less, win more and play with increased confidence. You'll learn the top 10 tips and winning strategies specifically designed for limit hold'em, no-limit hold'em, Omaha high-low and low-limit poker tournaments. Great practical advice for new players. 184 pages, $9.95..

I'M ALL IN: High Stakes, Big Business, and the Birth of the World Poker *Tour by Lyle Berman with Marvin Karlins.* Lyle Berman recounts how he revolutionized and revived the game of poker and transformed America's culture in the process. Get the inside story of the man who created the World Poker Tour, plus the exciting world of high-stakes gambling where a million dollars can be won or lost in a single game. Lyle reveals the 13 secrets of being a successful businessman, how poker players self-destruct, the 7 essential principles of winning at poker. Foreword by Donald Trump. Hardback, photos. 232 pages, $24.95.

7-CARD STUD: The Complete Course in Winning at Medium & Lower Limits *by Roy West.* Learn the latest strategies for winning at $1-$4 spread-limit up to $10/$20 fixed-limit games. Covers starting hands, 3rd-7th street strategy, overcards, selective aggressiveness, reading hands, pro secrets, psychology, and more in an informal 42 lesson format. Includes bonus chapter on 7-stud tournament strategy by Tom McEvoy. 224 pages, $19.95.

DOYLE BRUNSON'S EXCITING BOOKS
ADD THESE TO YOUR COLLECTION - ORDER NOW!

SUPER SYSTEM *by Doyle Brunson.* This classic book is considered by the pros to be the best book ever written on poker! Jam-packed with advanced strategies, theories, tactics and money-making techniques, no serious poker player can afford to be without this hard-hitting information. Includes fifty pages of the most precise poker statistics ever published. Features chapters written by poker's biggest superstars, such as Dave Sklansky, Mike Caro, Chip Reese, Joey Hawthorne, Bobby Baldwin, and Doyle. Essential strategies, advanced play, and no-nonsense winning advice on making money at 7-card stud (razz, high-low split, cards speak, and declare), draw poker, lowball, and hold'em (limit and no-limit).This is a must-read for any serious poker player. 628 pages, $29.95.

SUPER SYSTEM 2 *by Doyle Brunson.* The most anticipated poker book ever, SS2 expands upon the original with more games and professional secrets from the best in the world. Superstar contributors include Daniel Negreanu, winner of multiple WSOP gold bracelets and 2004 Poker Player of the Year; Lyle Berman, 3-time WSOP gold bracelet winner, founder of the World Poker Tour, and super-high stakes cash player; Bobby Baldwin, 1978 World Champion; Johnny Chan, 2-time World Champion and 10-time WSOP bracelet winner; Mike Caro, poker's greatest researcher, theorist, and instructor; Jennifer Harman, the world's top female player and one of ten best overall; Todd Brunson, winner of more than 20 tournaments; and Crandell Addington, no-limit hold'em legend. 672 pgs, $34.95.

CARO'S GUIDE TO DOYLE BRUNSON'S SUPER SYSTEM *by Mike Caro.* Working with World Champion Doyle Brunson, the legendary Mike Caro has created a fresh look to the "Bible" of all poker books, adding new and personal insights that help you understand the original work. Caro breaks 36 concepts into either "Analysis, Commentary, Concept, Mission, Play-By-Play, Psychology, Statistics, Story, or Strategy. Lots of illustrations and winning concepts give even more value to this great work. 86 pages, 8 1/2 x 11, $19.95.

ACCORDING TO DOYLE *by Doyle Brunson.* Learn what it takes to be a great poker player by climbing inside the mind of poker's most famous champion. Fascinating anecdotes and adventures from Doyle's early career playing poker in roadhouses are interspersed with lessons from the champion who has made more money at poker than anyone else in history. Learn what makes a great player tick, how he approaches the game, and receive candid, powerful advice from the legend himself. 208 pages, $14.95.

MY 50 MOST MEMORABLE HANDS *by Doyle Brunson.* This instant classic relives the most incredible hands by the greatest poker player of all time. Great players, legends, and poker's most momentous events march in and out of fifty years of unforgettable hands. Sit side-by-side with Doyle as he replays the excitement and life-changing moments of the most thrilling and crucial hands in the history of poker: from his early games as a rounder in the rough-and-tumble "Wild West" years—where a man was more likely to get shot as he was to get a straight flush—to the nail-biting excitement of his two world championship titles. Relive million dollar hands and the high stakes tension of sidestepping police, hijackers and murderers. A thrilling collection of stories and sage poker advice. 168 pages, $14.95.

ONLINE POKER *by Doyle Brunson.* Ten compelling chapters show you how to get started, explain the safety features which lets you play worry-free, and lets you in on the strategies that Doyle himself uses to beat players in cyberspace. Poker is poker, as Doyle explains, but there are also strategies that only apply to the online version, where the players are weaker!—and Doyle reveals them all in this book.192 pages, illustrations, $14.95.

BOBBY BALDWIN'S WINNING POKER SECRETS *by Mike Caro with Bobby Baldwin.* The fascinating account of 1978 World Champion Bobby Baldwin's early career playing poker against other legends is packed with valuable insights. Covers the common mistakes average players make at seven poker variations and the dynamic winning concepts needed for success. Endorsed by superstars Doyle Brunson and Amarillo Slim. 208 pages, $14.95.

MIKE CARO'S EXCITING WORK
POWERFUL BOOKS YOU __MUST__ HAVE

CARO'S MOST PROFITABLE HOLD'EM ADVICE *by Mike Caro.* When Mike Caro writes a book on winning, all poker players take notice. And they should: The "Mad Genius of Poker" has influenced just about every professional player and world champion alive. You'll journey far beyond the traditional tactical tools offered in most poker books and for the first time, have access to the entire missing arsenal of strategies left out of everything you've ever seen or experienced. Caro's first major work in two decades is packed with hundreds of powerful ideas, concepts, and strategies, many of which will be new to you—they have never been made available to the general public. This book represents Caro's lifelong research into beating the game of hold em. 408 pages, $24.95

MASTERING HOLD'EM AND OMAHA *by Mike Caro and Mike Cappelletti.* Learn the professional secrets to mastering the two most popular games of big-money poker: hold'em and Omaha. This is a thinking player's book, packed with ideas, with the focus is on making you a winning player. You'll learn everything from the strategies for play on the preflop, flop, turn and river, to image control and taking advantage of players stuck in losing patterns. You'll also learn how to create consistent winning patterns, use perception to gain an edge, avoid common errors, go after and win default pots, recognize and use the various types of raises, play marginal hands for profit, the importance of being loved or feared, and Cappelletti's unique point count system for Omaha. 328 pages, $19.95.

CARO'S BOOK OF POKER TELLS *by Mike Caro.* One of the ten greatest books written on poker, this must-have book should be in every player's library. If you're serious about winning, you'll realize that most of the profit comes from being able to read your opponents. Caro reveals the the secrets of interpreting *tells*—physical reactions that reveal information about a player's cards—such as shrugs, sighs, shaky hands, eye contact, and many more. Learn when opponents are bluffing, when they aren't and why—based solely on their mannerisms. Over 170 photos of players in action and play-by-play examples show the actual tells. These powerful ideas will give you the decisive edge. 320 pages, $24.95.

CARO'S FUNDAMENTAL SECRETS OF WINNING POKER *by Mike Caro.* Learn the essential strategies, concepts, and plays that comprise the very foundation of winning poker play. Learn to win more from weak players, equalize stronger players, bluff a bluffer, win big pots, where to sit against weak players, and the six factors of strategic table image. Includes selected tips on hold 'em, 7 stud, draw, lowball, tournaments, more. 160 pages, $12.95.

CARO'S PROFESSIONAL POKER REPORTS

Each of these three powerful insider poker reports is centered around a daily mission, with the goal of adding one weapon per day to your arsenal. Theoretical concepts and practical situations are mixed together for fast in-depth learning. For serious players.

11 DAYS TO 7-STUD SUCCESS. Bluffing, playing and defending pairs, different strategies for the different streets, analyzing situations—lots of information within. One advantage is gained each day. A quick and powerful method to 7-stud winnings. Essential. Signed, numbered. $19.95.

12 DAYS TO HOLD'EM SUCCESS. Positional thinking, playing and defending against mistakes, small pairs, flop situations, playing the river, are just some sample lessons. Guaranteed to make you a better player. Very popular. Signed, numbered. $19.95.

PROFESSIONAL 7-STUD REPORT. When to call, pass, and raise, playing starting hands, aggressive play, 4th and 5th street concepts, lots more. Tells how to read an opponent's starting hand, plus sophisticated advanced strategies. Important revision for serious players. Signed, numbered. $19.95.

THE CHAMPIONSHIP SERIES
POWERFUL INFORMATION YOU <u>MUST</u> HAVE

CHAMPIONSHIP NO-LIMIT & POT-LIMIT HOLD'EM *by T. J. Cloutier & Tom McEvoy.* The bible for winning pot-limit and no-limit hold'em tournaments gives you all the answers to your most important questions: How do you get inside your opponents' heads and learn how to beat them at their own game? How can you tell how much to bet, raise, and reraise in no-limit hold'em? When can you bluff? How do you set up your opponents in pot-limit hold'em so that you can win a monster pot? What are the best strategies for winning no-limit and pot-limit tournaments, satellites, and supersatellites? Rock-solid and inspired advice you can bank on from two of the most recognizable figures in poker. 304 pages, $29.95.

CHAMPIONSHIP HOLD'EM *by T. J. Cloutier & Tom McEvoy.* Hard-hitting hold'em the way it's played *today* in both limit cash games and tournaments. Get killer advice on how to win more money in rammin'-jammin' games, kill-pot, jackpot, shorthanded, and full table cash games. You'll learn the thinking process for preflop, flop, turn, and river play with specific suggestions for what to do when good or bad things happen. Includes play-by-play analyses, advice on how to maximize profits against rocks in tight games, weaklings in loose games, experts in solid games, plus tournament strategies for small buy-in, big buy-in, rebuy, add-on, satellite and big-field major tournaments. Wow! 392 pages, $29.95.

CHAMPIONSHIP OMAHA (Omaha High-Low, Pot-limit Omaha, Limit High Omaha) *by Tom McEvoy & T.J. Cloutier.* Clearly-written strategies and powerful advice from Cloutier and McEvoy who have won four World Series of Poker Omaha titles. You'll learn how to beat low-limit and high-stakes games, play against loose and tight opponents, and the differing strategies for rebuy and freezeout tournaments. Learn the best starting hands, when slowplaying a big hand is dangerous, what danglers are (and why winners don't play them), why you sometimes fold the nuts on the flop and would be correct in doing so, and overall, how you can win a lot of money at Omaha! 296 pages, illustrations, $29.95.

CHAMPIONSHIP HOLD'EM TOURNAMENT HANDS *by T. J. Cloutier & Tom McEvoy.* An absolute must for hold'em tournament players, two legends show you how to become a winning tournament player at both limit and no-limit hold'em games. Get inside the authors' heads as they think their way through the correct strategy at 57 limit and no-limit starting hands. Cloutier & McEvoy show you how to use skill and intuition to play strategic hands for maximum profit in real tournament scenarios and how 45 key hands were played by champions in turnaround situations at the WSOP. Gain tremendous insights into how tournament poker is played at the highest levels. 368 pages, $29.95.

CHAMPIONSHIP HOLD'EM SATELLITE STRATEGY *by Brad Dougherty & Tom McEvoy.* Every year satellite players win their way into the $10,000 WSOP buy-in and emerge as millionaires or champions. You can too! Learn the specific, proven strategies for winning almost any satellite from two world champions. Covers the ten ways to win a seat at the WSOP, how to win limit hold'em and no-limit hold'em satellites, one-table satellites, online satellites, and the final table of super satellites. Includes a special chapter on no-limit hold'em satellites! 320 pages, $29.95.

HOW TO WIN THE CHAMPIONSHIP: Hold'em Strategies for the Final Table, *by T.J. Cloutier.* If you're hungry to win a championship, this is the book that will pave the way! T.J. Cloutier, the greatest tournament poker player ever—he has won 60 major tournament titles and appeared at 39 final tables at the WSOP, both more than any other player in the history of poker—shows how to get to the final table where the big money is made and then how to win it all. You'll learn how to build up enough chips to make it through the early and middle rounds and then how to employ T.J.'s own strategies to outmaneuver opponents at the final table and win championships. You'll learn how to adjust your play depending upon stack sizes, antes/blinds, table position, opponents styles, chip counts, and the specific strategies for six-handed, three handed, and heads-up play. 288 pages, $29.95.

POWERFUL WINNING POKER SIMULATIONS
A MUST FOR SERIOUS PLAYERS WITH A COMPUTER!
IBM compatible CD ROM Win 95, 98, 2000, NT, ME, XP

These incredible full color poker simulations are the best method to improve your game. Computer opponents play like real players. All games let you set the limits and rake and have fully programmable players, plus stat tracking, and Hand Analyzer for starting hands. Mlke Caro, the world's foremost poker theoretician says, "Amazing... a steal for under $500... get it, it's great." Includes free phone support. "Smart Advisor" gives expert advice for every play!

1. TURBO TEXAS HOLD'EM FOR WINDOWS - $59.95. Choose which players, and how many (2-10) you want to play, create loose/tight games, and control check-raising, bluffing, position, sensitivity to pot odds, and more! Also, instant replay, pop-up odds, Professional Advisor keeps track of play statistics. Free bonus: Hold'em Hand Analyzer analyzes all 169 pocket hands in detail and their win rates under any conditions you set. Caro says this "hold'em software is the most powerful ever created." Great product!

2. TURBO SEVEN-CARD STUD FOR WINDOWS - $59.95. Create any conditions of play; choose number of players (2-8), bet amounts, fixed or spread limit, bring-in method, tight/loose conditions, position, reaction to board, number of dead cards, and stack deck to create special conditions. Features instant replay. Terrific stat reporting includes analysis of starting cards, 3-D bar charts, and graphs. Play interactively and run high speed simulation to test strategies. Hand Analyzer analyzes starting hands in detail. Wow!

3. TURBO OMAHA HIGH-LOW SPLIT FOR WINDOWS - $59.95. Specify any playing conditions; betting limits, number of raises, blind structures, button position, aggressiveness/passiveness of opponents, number of players (2-10), types of hands dealt, blinds, position, board reaction, and specify flop, turn, and river cards! Choose opponents and use provided point count or create your own. Statistical reporting, instant replay, pop-up odds high speed simulation to test strategies, amazing Hand Analyzer, and much more!

4. TURBO OMAHA HIGH FOR WINDOWS - $59.95. Same features as above, but tailored for Omaha High only. Caro says program is "an electrifying research tool...it can clearly be worth thousands of dollars to any serious player. A must for Omaha High players.

5. TURBO 7 STUD 8 OR BETTER - $59.95. Brand new with all the features you expect from the Wilson Turbo products: the latest artificial intelligence, instant advice and exact odds, play versus 2-7 opponents, enhanced data charts that can be exported or printed, the ability to fold out of turn and immediately go to the next hand, ability to peek at opponents hand, optional warning mode that warns you if a play disagrees with the advisor, and automatic mode that runs up to 50 tests unattended. Tough computer players vary their styles for a great game.

---

6. TOURNAMENT TEXAS HOLD'EM - $39.95

Set-up for tournament practice and play, this realistic simulation pits you against celebrity look-alikes. Tons of options let you control tournament size with 10 to 300 entrants, select limits, ante, rake, blind structures, freezeouts, number of rebuys and competition level of opponents. Pop-up status report shows how you're doing vs. the competition. Save tournaments in progress to play again later. Additional feature allows quick folds on finished hands.